I Love
DOGS

I Love DOGS

EDITED BY
PATRICIA M. SHERWOOD

LYONS
PRESS

Essex, Connecticut

An imprint of The Globe Pequot Publishing Group, Inc.
64 South Main Street
Essex, CT 06426
www.globepequot.com

Distributed by NATIONAL BOOK NETWORK

British Library Cataloguing in Publication Information available

Library of Congress Cataloging-in-Publication Data

Names: Sherwood, Patricia Miller editor
Title: I love dogs / edited by Patricia M. Sherwood.
Description: Essex, Connecticut : Lyons Press, [2025] | Includes index. | Summary: "I Love Dogs is a treasure trove of the wisest, funniest, and most heartwarming comments ever uttered about our beloved canine friends. It offers page after page of poignant observations on the training of dogs, the dog fancy, the joy and wonder dogs bring to our lives, the particularities of breeds, and the loss we feel when a dog has passed away"—Provided by publisher.
Identifiers: LCCN 2024059336 (print) | LCCN 2024059337 (ebook) | ISBN 9781493090426 paperback | ISBN 9781493090853 epub
Subjects: LCSH: Dogs—Quotations, maxims, etc.
Classification: LCC PN6084.D64 I55 2025 (print) | LCC PN6084.D64 (ebook) | DDC 636.7—dc23/eng/20250227
LC record available at https://lccn.loc.gov/2024059336
LC ebook record available at https://lccn.loc.gov/2024059337

♾️™ The paper used in this publication meets the minimum requirements of American National Standard for Information Sciences—Permanence of Paper for Printed Library Materials, ANSI/NISO Z39.48-1992.

CONTENTS

INTRODUCTION

Nowhere in the story is there any mention of Nagaicho, the
creator, creating a dog. Rather, when Nagaicho first started on
his walk, he took a dog with him: God already had a dog.

—STANLEY COREN, *THE INTELLIGENCE OF DOGS* [1994]

There are two hundred breeds of dogs registered with the American
Kennel Club, divided into seven groups: working, nonsporting, sporting, herding, terriers, toys, and hounds. Four more breeds are listed in
the miscellaneous class (including such exotics as the Polish lowland
sheepdog, Plott hound, spinone Italiano, and Jack Russell terrier). The
AKC alone registers well over a million puppies a year. And that's just
the beginning.

Nearly 350 other breeds, with known bloodlines and stud books,
exist as well, bringing the total worldwide registration of established
breeds up to more than five hundred varieties, from African lion hound
to Zwergdackel. In every country of the world, special dogs are bred for
special purposes—and fit their niches very well. Some are raised with
sheep to live in the herd and protect them from predators; the dogs
think they are sheep. There are ferocious guard dogs, specialized hunting dogs—one breed gambols up and down on the shoreline to entice
curious ducks within gunshot—dogs who were bred for food or companionship or decoration.

No other species varies so widely in size and configuration as does the domestic dog. The mighty Irish wolfhound towers over the tiny chihuahua; the cumbersome Saint Bernard can weigh 250 pounds; a delicate Italian greyhound, a mere 10. Old English sheepdogs drip with coat; Chinese crested dogs, virtually no hair. There are blue dogs, spotted dogs, striped dogs, dogs of black and red and white and yellow and brown . . . and more.

There are dogs bred to find grouse, to retrieve ducks, to sniff out contraband plants at airports, to herd cows, to guide the blind, to attack the wrongdoer, to dig deep in the earth after vermin, to rest comfortably in master's sleeve, to keep milady's hands warm, to rescue snowbound travelers, to swim to and save drowning people . . .

Moreover, each breed has distinguishing personality traits. Dr. Myrna Milani says in *Dogsmart* (1988), "A particular dog's breeding, then, can imbue it with a strong sense of functions and a set of specific behavioral patterns in addition to a specific coat or eye color." Sporting dogs' instinct says to cover ground—and lots of it. Sight hounds—those bred to run—have deep chests and huge thigh muscles to propel them forward. Sheepherding dogs tend to be more than one color, making them easier to identify among the solid-colored sheep. Terriers are persistent; they don't give up their goal easily—a useful trait in a dog who must pursue his prey into its den, regardless of how the prey feels about that. Each breed has not only distinguishing physical traits but specialized personality characteristics, as well.

Those characteristics, unique to each breed, attract unique owners: those who love the grace of a greyhound or the feistiness of a terrier or the single-minded devotion of a shepherd. Someone will say with pride, "I'm a terrier man," or, "I'm in wolfhounds," and they usually are, right up to the ears. They tend to be obsessive about their breed; read up on its history; keep track of trends in disease; consult web pages; meet frequently at specialty shows to brag and disparage; and have homes full of paintings, photographs, and statuary—all of their breed. MacKinlay Kantor said in *The Voice of Bugle Ann* (1935), "You see, sir, it's a matter of breeding good dogs—and understanding them—and kind of loving them."

That's the professional dog person. For the ordinary person, one dog at a time is enough. Enough to grow up with, to know, to be amused by, to get occasionally angry with, to observe, to love, and finally to mourn. Willie Morris says, "The dog of your boyhood teaches you a great deal about friendship, and love, and death: Old Skip was my brother." His autobiography, *My Dog Skip*, is largely centered on his dog.

The bond between man and dog is like no other. Elizabeth von Arnim in her *All the Dogs of My Life*, feels, though parents, husbands, children, lovers, and friends are all very well, they are not dogs. From the time the wolf moved into the caveman's stronghold in a symbiotic relationship of hunting and guarding, dogs have served, adored, worked for, entertained, and warmed man's heart. And man has responded with equal respect, responsibility, and affection. Mostly.

There are, of course, responses like that of Jean Kerr, who says in *Please Don't Eat the Daisies*, "I never meant to say anything about this, but the fact is that I have never met a dog that didn't have it in for me." Or the faint-praise damning of Emily Dickinson, who wrote a friend, "I think Carlo would please you. He is dumb, and brave." Stanley Bing wrote an article called "The Most Beautiful Girl in the World" (1990), in which he notes, "She's the sweetest dog in the world. . . . But she's got an IQ somewhere between a brick and a houseplant." He was not referring to his wife. Not everyone is entirely infatuated with their canine companion.

There is, however, a universality of feeling about dogs, when human and animal are in it together, whether it's working, hunting, or simply sitting around the fire. A herding-dog owner and exhibitor of my acquaintance said of working her dog, "It gives you something to talk about with your dog." Gary Paulsen felt so strongly about his sled dogs the emotion burst out of him: "I was complete, and part of that completeness was that we, the team and I, were in some way doing what we were meant to do." And more peacefully, Walt Whitman longed for "[f]alling asleep on the gather'd leaves, with my dog and gun by my side."

It's not only those who do something with their dogs who find them irreplaceable; it's also those of us who have a dog because we can't bear not to, those whose ownership (if one can call it that) is part and parcel of our being, who need a dog. Our name is legion. Pam Houston in *Waltzing the Cat* (1998) says, "I am dogless for the moment but it's not my natural condition."

The diversity of people who have not only owned dogs but who've also felt compelled to write something about them is just amazing. St. Augustine had a comment, ancient Greeks and Romans made observations, and writers from Chaucer to P. G. Wodehouse have looked upon dogs and put down their feelings. Who would have expected to find a long and adulatory essay by Thomas Mann on his dog—or comments from Woodrow Wilson or a quote from T. S. Eliot or words of praise from Robert Frost? As universal is man's feeling about dogs, so is the impulse to write about them or talk about them or include them in verse. Dogs get close to the heart and require their owners to express their feelings. And so from Winston Churchill to Anne Tyler to Aeschylus, they do so.

Surprisingly, many of the most lyrical writers are not "dog people"—they are simply people who have loved a dog. The wish to urge onto others the particular and unique charms of your dog is universal. The emotional response to canine friendship is the same for us all, even though for some there is a kind of rueful awareness that we see ourselves in our dogs' eyes as we would like to be—noble, worthy of adoration, the source of all good things, God.

It seemed appropriate to create a section of this book just for feelings—the emotions that dogs evoke, positive and not so—and one that pointed up the usage of dogs and canine imagery in our language. There was the need for some category that collected observations on behavior and characteristics—of both dogs and the people who own them. The dogs had to be allowed a chance to speak for themselves, to give the other side of the story. And no dog book would be complete without a section on dog shows and the unusual characters found there—and along with that, some grouping that limns at least a few of the breeds and their individual charms. There are sections for the special and delightful quotes about hunting dogs and hounds and working dogs. And finally, there is a place for the universal grief of losing a dog.

If you have ever been owned by a dog or reached down to pat one's head or admired one from a distance even, then I believe you will find some words in here that touch a note in you.

Patricia M. Sherwood

FEELINGS

My father worshipped dogs, hunting, fishing, the state of Maine, and the complete works of William Shakespeare, in that order.

—SUSAN CONANT, *TRUE CONFESSIONS* (1995)

We all respond emotionally to dogs: sometimes with curiosity, sometimes with fear or dislike, sometimes with anger or amusement or disbelief—and sometimes with love. A surprising variety of people have made note of their emotional responses, from Anatole France to Christopher Morley to Thorstein Veblen.

The first quotation here is by Marjorie Garber; the last, by an anonymous writer. In between are expressions of emotional response by several dozen other writers—all of whom wanted to set down their feelings about dogs.

Where today can we find the full panoply of William
Bennett's *Book of Virtues*—from Courage and Responsibility
to Loyalty and Family Values—but in Lassie and
Beethoven and Millie and Checkers and Spot.

—MARJORIE GARBER, *DOG LOVE* (1996)

I quickly found that with dogs, with running them, it is no hands for
the musher and all hands, eyes, mind, soul—everything for the dogs.

—GARY PAULSEN, *WINTERDANCE* (1994)

Dogs are . . . wonderful. Truly. To know them and be
with them is an experience that transcends—a way to
understand the joyfulness of living and devotion.

—GARY PAULSEN, *WINTERDANCE* (1994)

An animal is, properly speaking, a soul; I do not say an immortal
soul. And yet, when I come to consider the positions this
poor little beast and I myself occupy in the scheme of things,
I recognize in both exactly the same right to immortality.

—ANATOLE FRANCE, "THE COMING OF RIQUET" (1926)

The reactions of a country-house party to an after-dinner
dogfight in the drawing-room always vary considerably
according to the individual natures of its members.

—P. G. WODEHOUSE, *BLANDINGS CASTLE* (1935)

I love dogs, . . . but somehow the problems my houseplants have
presented in recent years have made me reluctant to take on
anything else that requires being considered when I travel.

—ANN BEATTIE, "CONSIDERATIONS (IN MIDDLE
AGE) CONCERNING GETTING A DOG" (1995)

He should have got a dog. Instead, he discovered vodka.

—SUSAN CONANT, *TRUE CONFESSIONS* (1995)

What's so good about uncritical, uncompromising, unconditional love?
Speaking for myself, if anyone, or anything, loves me, I'm only going to
feel good about it if I'm loved for my qualities—or anyway, a quality.

—DANIEL PINKWATER, "A WALK WITH JACQUES" (1995)

He was the doggiest dog anyone ever saw, just the way you can say that a Mexican-Yankee-Frenchman-Greek is the most Mexican-Yankee-Frenchman-Greek individual you ever saw, summing up all of himself as such, up to his cocky wonderful ears in whatever he is doing. This fellow was everything a creature could possibly be of HIM, of HE. He was Boss Dog.

—M. F. K. FISHER, *THE BOSS DOG* (1991)

I can only conclude that the legendary Jock fooled my mother into mistaking him for something other than what he was, perhaps a liver-and-white-ticked chair or an oddly hairy person.

—SUSAN CONANT, *TRUE CONFESSIONS* (1995)

So far in my life I've had only a few friends as satisfactory
as Jacques—and half of those friends have been dogs.
—DANIEL PINKWATER, "A WALK WITH JACQUES" (1995)

Sure, I've run into several dogs I was wary of, and one or two whose
personal habits have put me off—incessant and annoying barking,
or an obsession with the human knee—but by and large my major
impulse, when I see a dog, is to stop whatever I'm doing and say hello.
—STEVEN BAUER, "TAKE THAT, WILL ROGERS" (1995)

Much has been written about the loyalty of dogs,
but what I love about them isn't their devotion to
me so much as their devotion to being alive.
—STEVEN BAUER, "TAKE THAT, WILL ROGERS" (1995)

Dogs are not our whole life, but they make our lives whole.

—ROGER A. CARAS (1928-2001), NATURALIST

Thorns may hurt you, men desert you,

Sunlight turn to fog;

But you're never friendless ever,

If you have a dog.

—DOUGLAS MALLOCH, "IF YOU HAVE A DOG"

If You Have a Dog

. . . Behold

The fierce, blood-trailing wolf-pack's

progeny:

Man's friend and chum, the dog against your knee.

—STANTON A. COBLENTZ, "HERITAGE" (1946)

And the Woman said, "His name is not Wild Dog
any more, but the First Friend, because he will be
our friend for always and always and always."

—RUDYARD KIPLING, *JUST SO STORIES* (1902)

Nevertheless it is hardly fair
To risk your heart for a dog to tear.

—RUDYARD KIPLING, "THE POWER OF THE DOG" (1909)

All I observed was the silliness of the King, playing with
his dogs all the while and not minding the business.
—SAMUEL PEPYS, *DIARY, SEPTEMBER* (1666)

[T]he only piece of dog memorabilia she left was a clipping of a
classified ad that she placed. . . . It reads: "My husband's fifty-dollar
puppies for twenty-five dollars. If a man answers, hang up."
—SUSAN CONANT, *TRUE CONFESSIONS* (1995)

Liking children and dogs too much is a substitution for loving adults.
—JEAN-PAUL SARTRE, *WORDS* (1964)

He will hold thee. . . . Something better than
his dog, a little dearer than his horse.

—ALFRED, LORD TENNYSON, "LOCKSLEY HALL" (1842)

I loathe people who keep dogs. They are cowards who haven't got the guts to bite people themselves.

—AUGUST STRINDBERG, *INFERNO* (1897)

What she failed to grasp, he argued—one more principle he still hadn't drummed into her head—was that a dog is always going to act like a dog. That, said my mother, was exactly what she didn't like about them.

—SUSAN CONANT, *TRUE CONFESSIONS* (1995)

My love of dogs was, to a certain extent, an inborn trait; owing its origin to the laws of heredity.

—HARDING COX, *A SPORTSMAN AT LARGE* (1925)

The censure of a dog is something no man can stand.

—CHRISTOPHER MORLEY, *THE HAUNTED BOOKSHOP* (1919)

The more I see of men, the more I admire dogs.

—MADAME ROLAND (1754-1793), WRITER

And still I like to fancy that,

Somewhere beyond the Styx's bound,

Sir Guy's tall phantom stoops to pat

His little phantom hound.

—PATRICK R. CHALMERS, "HOLD" (1912)

As I get older, I feel myself becoming more and more a dog,

and I feel my dog becoming more and more an aristocrat.

—PAUL CLAUDEL (1868-1955), POET AND DRAMATIST

No one appreciates the very special genius of
your conversation as a dog does.

—CHRISTOPHER MORLEY (1890-1957), JOURNALIST AND NOVELIST

I never meant to say anything about this, but the fact is that
I have never met a dog that didn't have it in for me.

—JEAN KERR, *PLEASE DON'T EAT THE DAISIES* (1957)

The point is simple: a dog's capacity to inflate the ego of his
owner is almost nil. His capacity to irk him, inconvenience
him, put him at odds with his family and himself, and
generally embarrass and belittle him is almost unbounded.

—ROGER ANGELL, "LIVING WITH A DOG" (1951)

There is no man so poor but what he can afford to keep one dog.
And I have seen them so poor that they could afford to keep three.
—JOSH BILLINGS (1818-1885), HUMORIST

Yes, I am suffering from dogophobia. Only the
possession of a whole dog will cure me.
—BURGES JOHNSON, "CONFESSIONS OF A MAN
WHO DOESN'T OWN A DOG" (1877)

You ask of my companions. Hills, sir, and the sundown, and a
dog as large as myself that my father bought me. They are better
than human beings, because they know but do not tell.
—EMILY DICKINSON (1830-1886), POET

Oh, what is the matter with poor Puggy-wug?

Pet him and kiss him and give him a hug.

Run and fetch him a suitable drug,

Wrap him up tenderly all in a rug,

That is the way to cure Puggy-wug.

—WINSTON CHURCHILL, "POOR PUGGY-WUG" (1967)

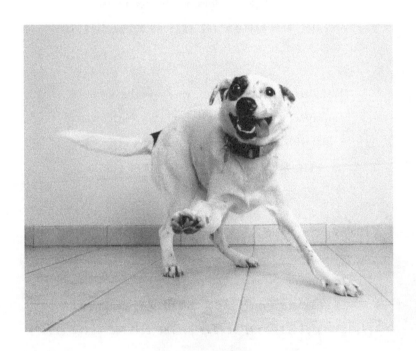

She's the sweetest dog in the world. . . . But she's got an

IQ somewhere between a brick and a houseplant.

—STANLEY BING, "THE MOST BEAUTIFUL

GIRL IN THE WORLD" (1990)

Watching Arnold run flat-out in a large open space
was unforgettable, and opened a window to something
exceedingly ancient and precious—a link to the first
time men followed dogs, and hunted to live.

—DANIEL PINKWATER, "THE SOUL OF A DOG" (1989)

●

Recollect that the Almighty, who gave the dog to be
companion of our pleasures and our toils, hath invested
him with a nature noble and incapable of deceit.

—SIR WALTER SCOTT, *THE TALISMAN* (1825)

●

The dog . . . commends himself to our favor by affording play to
our propensity for mastery, and as he is also an item of expense,
and commonly serves no industrial purpose, he holds a well-
assured place in men's regard as a thing of good repute.

—THORSTEIN VEBLEN, *THE THEORY OF THE LEISURE CLASS* (1899)

You can say any fool thing to a dog, and the dog will give you this look that says, "My God, you're right! I never would have thought of that!"

—DAVE BARRY (B. 1947), AUTHOR AND COLUMNIST

●

[I]n his human incarnation, he was probably an entrepreneur, inventor, or performance artist.

—BETTY FISHER AND SUZANNE DELZIO,
SO YOUR DOG'S NOT LASSIE (1998)

These are dandy things, I know—

But give a boy a dawg.

—DOUGLAS MALLOCH, "GIVE A BOY A DAWG" (1946)

The most unaccountable part of the conduct of the lower classes of
people in many parishes and which can be least easily reconciled
to the hardships of their situation, is their fondness for dogs.

—SIR JOHN SINCLAIR, *STATISTICAL ACCOUNT OF SCOTLAND* (1791)

I think that college dogs deserve to be reckoned as a separate
class. . . . [A]t my own college it was estimated that each
member of the college had a dog and a third, while in
another college two dogs and a quarter was the average.

—REVEREND J. G. WOOD,
THE ILLUSTRATED NATURAL HISTORY [1851]

A good man will take care of his horses and dogs, not only
while they are young, but when old and past service.

—PLUTARCH, *SYMPOSIACA* [C. 100 AD]

Jim Thurber once remarked, "I am not a dog-lover. To me,
a dog-lover is a dog who is in love with another dog."

—JACK GOODMAN, *THE FIRESIDE BOOK OF DOG STORIES* [1943]

In 1576 [in France] the annual budget for royal dogs
reached the sum of 100,000 gold crowns.

—FERNAND MÉRY,

THE LIFE, HISTORY AND MAGIC OF THE DOG (1970)

In some times and places people have viewed dogs as loyal,
faithful, noble, intelligent, courageous, and sociable; in other
eras and locations, humans have thought dogs cowardly,
unclean, disease ridden, dangerous, and unreliable.

—STANLEY COREN, THE INTELLIGENCE OF DOGS (1994)

The two local dogs are . . . a golden cocker, and . . .
a black Labrador. . . . Both are far more intelligent
than a Christian, or at least than a clergyman.

—REVEREND J. G. WOOD,

THE ILLUSTRATED NATURAL HISTORY (1851)

There are three faithful friends—an old wife,
an old dog, and ready money.

—BENJAMIN FRANKLIN, POOR RICHARD'S ALMANACK (1733-1758)

At least two of them have understood simple English, more or less, or at any rate have put on an intelligent expression when spoken to. (I remember using the same trick as a schoolboy when interrupted in my daydreams.)

—ALEC GUINNESS, *A POSITIVELY FINAL APPEARANCE* (1999)

[I]f I don't understand his words, spoken with the intensity of haiku, he, like a boorish American on vacation in Europe, barks louder.

—KAREN DOWELL, *COOKING WITH DOGS* (1998)

For it is by muteness that a dog becomes for one so utterly beyond value; with him one is at peace, where words play no torturing tricks.

—JOHN GALSWORTHY, *MEMORIES* [1912]

Why is it sometimes easier to say "I love my dog" than "I love my spouse"?

—MARJORIE GARBER, *DOG LOVE* [1996]

What worser place can I beg in your love
(And yet a place of high respect with me)
Than to be used as you use your dog?

—WILLIAM SHAKESPEARE, *A MIDSUMMER NIGHT'S DREAM* [1600]

[F]or anyone who has ever owned a dog, loved a dog, wanted to wring a dog's neck or wishes the dog would take a long weekend.

—VINCENT CANBY (1924-2000), AMERICAN FILM CRITIC

I think Carlo would please you. He is dumb, and brave.

—EMILY DICKINSON, LETTER TO THOMAS
WENTWORTH HIGGINSON (1862)

The eyes of a dog, the expression of a dog, the warmly wagging tail of a dog and the gloriously cold damp nose of a dog were in my opinion all God-given for one purpose only—to make complete fools of us human beings.

—BARBARA WOODHOUSE, NO BAD DOGS (1982)

I never understand what you're barking at when nothing's there.

—KAREN DOWELL, COOKING WITH DOGS (1998)

The dog of your boyhood teaches you a great deal about friendship, and love, and death: Old Skip was my brother.

—WILLIE MORRIS, MY DOG SKIP (1995)

She worshipped my wife and slept beside the bed when I was gone, and would I am certain have died in defence of the household with the same driven ferocity she showed in combat with wild things.

—JOHN GRAVES, *BLUE AND SOME OTHER DOGS* (1981)

Dogs are at the best no more than verminous vagrants, self-scratchers, foul feeders, and unclean by the law of Moses and Mohammed; but a dog with whom one lives alone for at least six months in the year; a free thing, tied to you so strictly by love that without you he will not stir or exercise; a patient, temperate, humorous, wise soul, who knows your moods before you know them yourself, is not a dog under any ruling.

—RUDYARD KIPLING, "GARM-A HOSTAGE" (1899)

It is true that whenever a person loves a dog he derives great power from it. Dogs still know all we say, only they are not at liberty to speak. If you do not love a dog, he has the power to injure you with his orenda [magic].

—SENECA FOLKTALE

It was quite hard to stay angry at a large strong dog, no matter what he had just done, who had his bobtailed butt in the air and his head along his forelegs on the ground and his eyes skewed sidewise at you as he smiled a wide, mad, minstrel-show smile.

—JOHN GRAVES, *BLUE AND SOME OTHER DOGS* (1981)

Today you, a sober character, an early riser, you are the right master for that stout hunter who has just cleared the railings again out of sheer joy in the fact that today you apparently belong to him alone and not to the world.

—THOMAS MANN, *BASHAN AND I* (1918)

Dogs naturally run in packs, following the strongest personalities therein as leaders thereof. Your pup takes you for the lead dog. So you behave, hear? Don't mess up your image.

—L. M. BOYD (1927-2007), COLUMNIST

You see, sir, it's a matter of breeding good dogs—and understanding them—and kind of loving them.

—MACKINLAY KANTOR, *THE VOICE OF BUGLE ANN* (1935)

We are alone, absolutely alone on this chance planet;
and amid all the forms of life that surround us, not one,
excepting the dog, has made an alliance with us.

—MAURICE MAETERLINCK, *OUR FRIEND, THE DOG* (1904)

Dog, n. A kind of additional or subsidiary Deity designed to
catch the overflow and surplus of the world's worship.

—AMBROSE BIERCE, *THE DEVIL'S DICTIONARY* (1906)

The one absolutely unselfish friend that man can have in
this selfish world, the one that never deserts him, the one
that never proves ungrateful or treacherous, is his dog.

—SAMUEL TAYLOR COLERIDGE, *TABLE-TALK* (1830)

Dogs never lie about love.

—MIKE DEL ROSSO (1948-2023), DISC JOCKEY

In the beginning, God created man, but seeing
him so feeble, He gave him the dog.

—ALPHONSE TOUSSENEL (1803-1885), WRITER AND JOURNALIST

I would like, to begin with, to say that though parents, husbands,
children, lovers and friends are all very well, they are not dogs.

—ELIZABETH VON ARNIM (1866-1941), NOVELIST

For perhaps, if the truth were known, we're all a little blind, a little deaf, a little handicapped, a little lonely, a little less than perfect. And if we can learn to appreciate and utilize the dog's full potentials, we will, together, make it in this life on earth.

—CHARLOTTE SCHWARTZ,
FRIEND TO FRIEND: DOGS THAT HELP MANKIND (1984)

Then the sun god decided to create new people. First he made a man, then a woman, and finally a dog to keep them company.

—TEHUELCHE FOLKTALE

It is a sobering thought that cats and dogs are more loyal,
trustworthy, and reliable than human beings.

—DESMOND MORRIS, *DOGWATCHING* (1986)

Bix . . . is built like a cinder block. He is one of those
nice, genial, somewhat slow-witted creatures, without the
brain-size to conceive dishonest or malicious thoughts.
I know people like that, and treasure them, too.
—VANCE BOURJAILY, *COUNTRY MATTERS* (1973)

On the other hand I distrust people who believe that dogs are better
than we are. Dogs are not better. They are just different from us.
Surely they can do some things better, but I have yet to see a dog
balance a checkbook, or make an omelette or compose a sonnet.
—JOHN STEINBECK, A LETTER EXPLAINING WHY HE
COULD NOT WRITE AN INTRODUCTION FOR TED PATRICK'S
BOOK, *THE THINKING MAN'S DOG* (1964)

She had become more than a friend—almost an
alter ego—in the year of trapping and work.
—GARY PAULSEN, *WINTERDANCE* (1994)

I thought my whole life had changed, that I wasn't sure if I
would ever recover, that I had seen god and he is a dog-man.
—GARY PAULSEN, *WINTERDANCE* (1994)

Is it true that there is a silly school which holds that a dog has no memory? I wonder how they arrived at that staggering generality. If they said it about me, it would be more to the point.

—JOHN STEINBECK, A LETTER EXPLAINING WHY HE COULD NOT WRITE AN INTRODUCTION FOR TED PATRICK'S BOOK, *THE THINKING MAN'S DOG* (1964)

[T]he old joke about how you can tell a bride at a WASP wedding: "She's the one kissing the golden retriever."

—MARJORIE GARBER, *DOG LOVE* (1996)

Whoever said you can't buy happiness forgot about puppies.
—GENE HILL (1928-1997), AUTHOR

[Y]ou must 'ave noo laid heggs for your homlets,
and cream for your spanil dog.
—WILLIAM MAKEPEACE THACKERAY, *VANITY FAIR* (1848)

They are playful companions when we are in the mood for fun;
they are loving companions when we are lonely or depressed; they
are health-giving companions when they spur us into taking long
walks; they are calming companions when we become agitated,
apprehensive, or tense; and they still carry out their age-old duties
of alerting us to intruders in our homes and protecting us from
attack—to mention only two of their surviving work roles.
—DESMOND MORRIS, *DOGWATCHING* (1986)

[T]he knowledge, the absolute fundamental knowledge that
I could not stop, would not stop, would never be able to stop
running dogs of my own free will . . . because I wanted to see the
beauty again, find the wonderful places they would take me.

—GARY PAULSEN, *WINTERDANCE* (1994)

He is your friend, your partner, your defender, your dog. You are his
life, his love, his leader. He will be yours, faithful and true, to the last
beat of his heart. You owe it to him to be worthy of such devotion.

—ANONYMOUS

OBSERVATIONS

Dogs can sigh very markedly. . . . Dogs sigh when, after having great expectations, they finally give up hope that the expected will happen.

—GÖRAN BERGMAN, *WHY DOES YOUR DOG DO THAT?* (1970)

One can't spend much time around dogs without noticing what they do—and trying to figure out why. They can be awfully funny. And often very human. They hate the vet, love the car, distrust the mailman. They do odd things. And they make us smile. Their behaviors are as varied as the authors who've pondered the phenomena.

The people around dogs also lend themselves to observation and conclusion. Usually the dogs come off better.

Dream dog leaps out of the moon with nothing
in its muzzle but bones of yellow light.
—LOUIS PHILLIPS, "DREAM DOG" (1983)

Across cold, moon-bright
distant stillness, a dog barks,
and then another.
—HARRY BEHN, "AUTUMN" (1984)

Sweet dogs, sour dogs, dogs that wagged and bit at the same
time, dogs that wouldn't be happy unless they had a finger to eat,
dogs that just lay down and looked at you when you harnessed
them, dogs that loved to run, hated to run, dogs that made war,
dogs that gave up and some, rare ones, who never, ever did.
Dogs like people.
—GARY PAULSEN, *WINTERDANCE* (1994)

It is probably true, then, that dogs don't think about
art, the origin of the universe, or geopolitics.

—ROGER A. CARAS, *A DOG IS LISTENING* (1992)

For the sake of simplicity, we'll divide dogs
into friendly and unfriendly dogs.

—J. J. MCCOY, *HOW TO LIVE WITH A DOG* (1962)

Most dogs are terribly informal creatures. They do things in
company that we would only do in private. In fact, they do
things in company that we would not do, even in private—
this is true of me, anyway, and I hope of the reader.

—DANIEL PINKWATER, "A WALK WITH JACQUES" (1995)

Dog owners spend a great deal of time looking down. That is because the production, cleanup and analysis of stools is a very important component of maintaining a healthy dog.

—CONNIE VANACORE, *DOG SHOWING* (1990)

Outside of a dog, a book is man's best friend.
Inside of a dog it's too dark to read.

—GROUCHO MARX (1890-1977), COMEDIAN AND ACTOR

"A parakeet is nice, like a feather on a hat," she
always said, . . . "but a dog is a mensch."
—ENID SHOMER, "MR. AND MRS. FOO" (1995)

I believe a smart man is probably superior to a smart dog.
—JOHN STEINBECK, *TRAVELS WITH CHARLEY* (1962)

Dogs have long endured a shaky, distrustful relationship with cars.
A loved one carried off, a trip to the vet, motion sickness, even
the specter of sudden death—these are only a few of the memories
that contribute to a deep unease in or around automobiles.
—DANNY SHANAHAN, "HOW TO READ YOUR DOG" (1995)

Why, a dog, when he sees a stranger, is angry; when an acquaintance he welcomes him, although the one has never done him any harm, not the other any good.

—PLATO, *THE REPUBLIC* (C. 375 BC)

Road notice to foreign tourists, Japan, 1935:

Give big space

to the festive dog

that makes sport

in the road-way.

Avoid entanglement of dog

with your wheel-spokes.

—WILLIAM LEAST HEAT-MOON, *RIVER-HORSE* (1999)

[Demonstrably], the best device for handling all of these complex elements of existence is intelligence, thinking. . . . We have been steadily evolving the capacity in our species, and I know of not a single shred of evidence that would demonstrate that dogs haven't been doing the same thing, albeit at a different rate, in different ways, to different levels to solve sometimes, but only sometimes, different problems.

—ROGER A. CARAS, *A DOG IS LISTENING* (1992)

[T]here was nothing he enjoyed more . . . than a
good book. He'd wander into the study, take down
some leather-bound volume, and eat it.

—TERENCE BRADY, "BOBBY'S MAIN VICE WAS ORGIES"

Sir, he's a good dog, and a fair dog; can there be more said?

—WILLIAM SHAKESPEARE, *THE MERRY WIVES OF WINDSOR* [1602]

The dog whom Fate had granted to behold

His lord, when twenty tedious years had roll'd,

Takes a last look, and, having seen him, dies;

So closed forever faithful Argus' eyes.

—HOMER, *THE ODYSSEY* (EIGHTH CENTURY BC)

If a dog will not come to you after he has looked you in the

face, you ought to go home and examine your conscience.

—WOODROW WILSON (1856-1924), US PRESIDENT

There is no doubt that every healthy, normal boy (if there is such

a thing in these days of Child Study) should own a dog at some

time in his life, preferably between the ages of 45 and 50.

—ROBERT BENCHLEY (1889-1945), HUMORIST

[I]n the circles I am speaking of, what "dear Fido" has done, does do, won't do, will do, can do, can't do, was doing, is going, is going to do, shan't do, and about to be going to have done, is the continual theme of discussion from morning till night.

—JEROME K. JEROME, "ON CATS AND DOGS" (1889)

I, personally, have no doubt that distinct mental processes do go on inside the dog's brain, although many times these processes are hardly worthy of the name.

—ROBERT BENCHLEY, *CHIPS OFF THE OLD BENCHLEY* (1949)

Dog wisdom is inside the blood and bones.

—DONALD MCCAIG (1940-2018), NOVELIST AND POET

Ninety-five percent of the . . . dogs in this country are flea
bags and affectionate parasites. For nothing more than a little
companionship, a wag of the tail, they get room and board, medical
care, social security, plush living, unemployment compensation,
plus your easy chair. What kind of a business deal is that?

—RICHARD A. WOLTERS, *GUN DOG* (1961)

My dog can bark like a congressman, fetch like an aide, beg like a press
secretary and play dead like a receptionist when the phone rings.

—GERALD SOLOMON (1930-2001), CONGRESSMAN

I am his Highness' dog at Kew,

Pray tell me, sir, whose dog are you?

—ALEXANDER POPE, ENGRAVED ON THE COLLAR OF A
DOG HE GAVE TO FREDERICK, PRINCE OF WALES

Let dogs delight to bark and bite,

For God hath made them so.

—ISAAC WATTS, "SONG XVI. AGAINST
QUARRELLING AND FIGHTING" (1715)

Dogs will always present you with problems, conundrums, solutions.

—STEPHEN J. BODIO, *ON THE EDGE OF THE WILD* (1998)

Dogs are like boys. If a new boy, or a new dog, moves into
a neighborhood they all make excuses to come around
and see what he looks like, whether he will take an insult
or resent it, whether he will fight or turn and run.

—HAL BORLAND, *THE DOG WHO CAME TO STAY* (1961)

"[T]he curious incident of the dog in the nighttime."
"The dog did nothing in the nighttime."
"That was the curious incident," remarked Sherlock Holmes.

—SIR ARTHUR CONAN DOYLE,
THE MEMOIRS OF SHERLOCK HOLMES (1893)

We expect our dogs to listen to us when we speak to them and
our dogs, no less than we, do expect us to listen to them.

—ROGER A. CARAS, *A DOG IS LISTENING* (1992)

Such as that dog is, who by barking craves,
And quiets grows soon as his food he gnaws.

—DANTE ALIGHIERI, *THE DIVINE COMEDY* (1321)

As he who take a strange dog by the ears is likely to be bitten.

—GEOFFREY CHAUCER, *CANTERBURY TALES*
(LATE FOURTEENTH CENTURY)

[A] dog never lies, but when was a wolf known to speak the truth?

—JAMES FENIMORE COOPER, *LAST OF THE MOHICANS* (1826)

Dogs are wolves, although they sometimes look
like they are in sheep's clothing.

—BRUCE FOGLE (1944-1973), VETERINARIAN AND AUTHOR

If you're only interested in dogs as a food source, then the
question of their intelligence is moot. Who wants smart food?

—STANLEY COREN, *THE INTELLIGENCE OF DOGS* (1994)

If dogs could talk, perhaps we would find it as hard
to get along with them as we do with people.

—KAREL ČAPEK (1890-1938), WRITER AND PLAYWRIGHT

A dog is not "almost human" and I know of no greater
insult to the canine race than to describe it as such.

—JOHN HOLMES (1913-2000), WRITER

He was a faker and a showoff, and a furious barker
after anything which couldn't bark back.

—NORMAN CORWIN, *THE ODYSSEY OF RUNYON JONES* (1941)

For reasons that are probably clear to them alone, most dogs consider the insides of automobiles their private domain and will take stern measures to protect this area against intruders.

—STEPHEN BAKER, *HOW TO LIVE WITH A NEUROTIC DOG* (1960)

The dog was created especially for children. He is the god of frolic.

—HENRY WARD BEECHER (1813-1887), CLERGYMAN

"Where do dogs go?" once wrote Nestor Roqueplan in an immortal story he has probably forgotten. . . . Where do dogs go? you ask, you unmindful people. They go about their business.

—CHARLES BAUDELAIRE, *THE PARISIAN PROWLER* (1990)

The dogs on leashes were not much bother, but in the warm late-autumn air a great many masters, out for a digestive or perhaps merely meditative stroll after church-and-dinner (with the traditional Sunday treat of little cakes from the pastry shop at the corner), had loosened not only their belts but their discipline, and as everybody knows, lower-class animals if given an inch will take a mile.

—M. F. K. FISHER, *THE BOSS DOG* (1991)

[T]he spectator dogs lie along the fence like so many silent torpedoes watching every move.

—DONALD MCCAIG, *A USEFUL DOG* (2004)

[I]f that ball were really lost, then indeed he took over
the proceedings with an intensity and quiet vigor that
destroyed many shrubs, and the solemn satisfaction which
comes from being in the very centre of the stage.

—JOHN GALSWORTHY, *MEMORIES* (1912)

He was certainly no Christian; but, allowing for
essential dog, he was very much a gentleman.

—JOHN GALSWORTHY, *MEMORIES* (1912)

The mind of a dog doesn't look into the future if its sex organs
are to be removed; it doesn't anticipate a loss of pleasure.

—MARJORIE GARBER, *DOG LOVE* (1996)

The dog . . . cannot answer questions as to whether his sex life is
normal or whether he had unpleasant sexual adventures when young.

—BARBARA WOODHOUSE (1910-1988), TRAINER AND AUTHOR

Neuter? You mean . . . cut their balls off? Why would I cut their
balls off? I wouldn't let nobody cut my balls off, and my dogs are
my best friends—why would I let someone cut their balls off?

—GERALD MCCLELLAN (B. 1967), MIDDLEWEIGHT BOXER

Man himself cannot express love and humility by external signs
so plainly as does a dog, when with dropping ears, hanging lips,
flexuous body, and wagging tail, he meets his beloved master.

—CHARLES DARWIN (1809-1882), NATURALIST AND GEOLOGIST

If ever the world's diplomats and arms negotiators learn
the spaniel gaze there will be peace on earth.

—LARRY SHOOK, *THE PUPPY REPORT* (1994)

Thou shalt not bring the hire of a whore, or the
price of a dog, into the house of the Lord.

—DEUTERONOMY 23:18

I am easily moved to sympathy for dogs, far more so than for humans, because dogs do not understand. There is no way to explain that you will return, that the vet will make it all better, that they cannot come shooting today because that is not what today is about. They cannot work out that their misery is finite and will some time end, and so their misery is magnified.

—GERALD HAMMOND, *MAD DOGS AND SCOTSMEN* (1995)

The dog can do many things which man cannot do, never could do and never will do.

—JOHN HOLMES, *THE FARMER'S DOG* (1960)

He had a terrible, terrible necessity to love, and this trammelled
the native, savage hunting beast which he was.

—D. H. LAWRENCE, "REX" (1921)

When the long winter nights come on and the wolves follow their
meat into the lower valleys, he may be seen running at the head
of the pack through the pale moonlight or glimmering borealis,
leaping gigantic above his fellows, his great throat a-bellow as
he sings of the younger world, which is the song of the pack.

—JACK LONDON, CALL OF THE WILD (1903)

[A] rag of wolf's tongue redpanting from his jaws.

—JAMES JOYCE, ULYSSES (1920)

As the sound dies away another animal takes it up, and then another
and another, until the hells re-echo with the same unutterably
dreary plaint. . . . It [is] evident that this is a solemn function—some
sacred rite which must be performed in these circumstances.

—ROBERT FALCON SCOTT, *THE VOYAGE OF THE DISCOVERY* (1905)

Our domestic dogs are descended from wolves and jackals
and though they may not have gained in cunning, and
may have lost in wariness and suspicion, yet they have
progressed in certain moral qualities, such as affection, trust-
worthiness, temper, and probably in general intelligence.

—CHARLES DARWIN,
THE DESCENT OF MAN, AND SELECTION IN RELATION TO SEX (1871)

All knowledge, the totality of all questions
and answers, is contained in the dog.

—FRANZ KAFKA, "INVESTIGATIONS OF A DOG" (1931)

And what a smile of attentive obligingness, of incorruptible innocence,
of affectionate submission, of boundless gratitude and total self-
abandonment lit up, at the least caress, that adorable mask of ugliness!

—MAURICE MAETERLINCK, OUR FRIEND, THE DOG (1904)

It is a deep-lying patriarchal instinct in a dog which leads him—at least in the more manly, outdoor breeds—to recognize and honour in the man of the house and head of the family his absolute master and overlord, protector of the hearth.

—THOMAS MANN, *BASHAN AND I* (1918)

Every dog is extremely susceptible to ridicule.

—R. H. SMYTHE, *THE MIND OF THE DOG* (1958)

Whatever threatens the human household
threatens the dog's world tenfold.

—DONALD MCCAIG, *NOP'S HOPE* (1994)

The pretty bitches put their noses in the cold water and lifted their heads to smile when they got out of breath drinking.

—THOMAS MCGUANE, *TO SKIN A CAT* (1986)

There is honor in being a dog.

—ARISTOTLE, *RHETORIC* (FOURTH CENTURY BC)

[S]nap up wisdom much as a dog snaps up a morsel?

—ARISTOPHANES, *THE CLOUDS* (423 BC)

It all comes of having a dog for a nurse.

—J. M. BARRIE, *PETER PAN* (1904)

Can a dog see with his nose?

—AMBROSE BIERCE, *THE DEVIL'S DICTIONARY* (1906)

Drive is what makes the dog chase the rabbit.

—JOEL MCMAINS, *DOG LOGIC* (1992)

If the old dog bark, he gives counsel.

—GEORGE HERBERT, *JACULA PRUDENTUM* (1651)

Dogs have been required to guard our homes, protect our persons, aid our hunts, destroy our vermin, and pull our sleighs. . . . They have been trained to collect birds' eggs in their mouths without breaking the shells, locate truffles, sniff out drugs at airports, guide the blind, rescue avalanche victims, track down escaped criminals, run races, travel in space, act in films, and compete as show dogs.

—DESMOND MORRIS, *DOGWATCHING* (1986)

An old Inuit belief states that dogs and white men
stem from the same roots because they cannot wait,
have no patience, and become frustrated easily.

—GARY PAULSEN, *WINTERDANCE* (1994)

But a most genteel and elegant little dog is infinitely
superior company to Cousin Tabitha Twitchit.

—BEATRIX POTTER, "THE PIE AND THE PATTYPAN" (1905)

To his dog, every man is Napoleon; hence the popularity of dogs.

—ALDOUS HUXLEY, *READER'S DIGEST* (1934)

A dog teaches a boy fidelity, perseverance, and to
turn around three times before lying down.

—ROBERT BENCHLEY, *READER'S DIGEST* (1963)

But this was beyond dispute an organized, concerted piece of showing-off that reminded me again how much like people dogs are: in their emotions if not in their reasoning ability.

—SPARSE GREY HACKLE, *AN HONEST ANGLER* (1998)

It seemed to me that a Long Island poodle who had made his devoirs to *Sequoia sempervirens* or *Sequoia gigantia* might be set apart from other dogs—might even be like that Galahad who saw the Grail. . . . A dog with an experience like that could become a pariah in the truest sense of the word.

—JOHN STEINBECK, *TRAVELS WITH CHARLEY* (1962)

His whole life, if he be a dog of any pretension to gallantry, is
spent in a vain show, and in the hot pursuit of admiration.
—ROBERT LOUIS STEVENSON, "THE CHARACTER OF DOGS" (1887)

Conceited whelp! we laugh at thee—
Nor mind, that not a few
Of pompous, two-legged dogs there be,
Conceited quite as you.
—ABRAHAM LINCOLN, "THE BEAR HUNT" (1847)

Bathed with sweet-smelling shampoo, brushed and
teased, de-matted and fluff-dried, cut and trimmed from
topknot to toenails, a well-groomed dog is more than just
a tour de force of cleanliness; it is a flight of fancy.
—JANE AND MICHAEL STERN, *DOG EAT DOG* (1997)

[H]e is a good watch dog—has a roar like a lion, designed
to conceal from night-wandering strangers the fact that
he couldn't bite his way out of a cornet de papier.
—JOHN STEINBECK, *TRAVELS WITH CHARLEY* (1962)

I am dogless for the moment but it's not my natural condition.

—PAM HOUSTON, *WALTZING THE CAT* [1998]

He was like the dog who would not leave the
place where his master is buried.

—JULES VERNE, *THE MYSTERIOUS ISLAND* [1875]

Blackie abandoned promiscuous begging and attached
himself to us as our permanent dog. His devotion
was exemplary and his appetite enormous.

—ERNEST HEMINGWAY, "THE CHRISTMAS GIFT" (1954)

Once he ceased hunting and became man's plate-licker, the
Rubicon was crossed. Thenceforth he was a gentleman of leisure;
and except the few whom we keep working, the whole race
grew more and more self-conscious, mannered and affected.

—ROBERT LOUIS STEVENSON, "THE CHARACTER OF DOGS" (1887)

When men are lonely, they stoop to any companionship;
the dog becomes a comrade, the horse a friend, and it is no
shame to shower them with caresses and speeches of love.

—LEW WALLACE, BEN-HUR (1880)

The dog has got more fun out of Man than Man has got
out of the dog, for the clearly demonstrable reason that
Man is the more laughable of the two animals.

—JAMES THURBER, THURBER'S DOGS (1955)

He is never more than half ashamed of having barked or
bitten; and for those faults into which he has been led by
the desire to shine before a lady of his race, he retains, even
under physical correction, a share of pride. But to be caught
lying, if he understands it, instantly uncurls his fleece.

—ROBERT LOUIS STEVENSON, "THE CHARACTER OF DOGS" (1887)

•

Like pigeons, dogs are supposed to have a supernatural ability to
find their way home across hundreds, even thousands, of miles
of strange terrain. The newspapers are full of dogs who have
miraculously turned up at the doorsteps of baffled masters who had
abandoned them afar. Against these stories, however, can be set
the lost and found columns of the same papers, which in almost
every issue carry offers of rewards for the recovery of dogs that,
apparently, couldn't find their way back from the next block.

—BERGEN EVANS, *THE NATURAL HISTORY OF NONSENSE* (1946)

The dog has seldom been successful in pulling man up to his level
of sagacity, but man has frequently dragged the dog down to his.

—JAMES THURBER, "SNAPSHOT OF A DOG" (1935)

The common wisdom is that men marry their
mothers and dogs look like their owners.

—CONNIE VANACORE, *DOG SHOWING* (1990)

Don't accept your dog's admiration as conclusive
evidence that you are wonderful.

—EPPIE LEDERER (ANN LANDERS) (1918-2002), ADVICE COLUMNIST

Dogs like to bark.
They like it best after dark.

—OGDEN NASH, "AN INTRODUCTION TO DOGS" (1936)

A door is what a dog is perpetually on the wrong side of.

—OGDEN NASH, "A DOG'S BEST FRIEND IS HIS ILLITERACY" (1949)

■ ■ ■ ■ ■ ■ ■ ■ ■

THE DOGS SPEAK

[S]he cocks her head to one side, fixes one with her luminous almond eyes, furrows her brow into puzzlement and seems to say, "I would understand you thoroughly if you could speak more clearly. And, incidentally, have you got a biscuit on you?"

—ALEC GUINNESS, *A POSITIVELY FINAL APPEARANCE* (1999)

It's no secret dogs can talk. It's less well known that they are often smart enough to find a human to write down what they say. It gives them a chance to give us their point of view—about fleas and the moon and people.

Of all the characters included here, my favorite is Dean Spanley, who revealed his previous incarnation as a dog under the influence of a rare tokay wine, which would have been much more interesting to hear than what most drunks have to say.

If a dog's prayers were answered, bones would rain from the sky.

—TURKISH PROVERB

•

"I want to go out!" "I want something to eat!" "Pet me, scratch me, rub my ears now!" Dogs go in for exclamation points.

—ARTHUR YORINKS, "THE EYES HAVE IT" (1995)

•

Most dogs have this idea running through their minds constantly: "Petme petme petme petme petme."

—BETTY FISHER AND SUZANNE DELZIO,
SO YOUR DOG'S NOT LASSIE (1998)

•

[T]here is always a certain thought-link between a dog and a cook, which occasionally can develop into quite a warm friendship.

—NOEL DE VIC BEAMISH, MISS PERFECTION (1931)

[A]ll the other questions dogs ask of the world they inhabit. What's in the bag? for example. Is it time for our walk yet? Did you hear that noise, stupid? Why so stingy with the wet food, fella?

—LEE K. ABBOTT, "TWENTY QUESTIONS" (1995)

Dogs don't trouble themselves with minutes or hours. Time is either "now!" or "right now!"

—ARTHUR YORINKS, "THE EYES HAVE IT" (1995)

Dogs, with their nose-to-the-ground, tail-wagging eagerness, their let-me-at-that-squirrel enthusiasm, remind me that what might on some days seem routine or dreary is only that way if you refuse to see the world at each moment with new eyes.

—STEVEN BAUER, "TAKE THAT, WILL ROGERS" (1995)

Dogs, he said, only asked two questions of the

world: Can I eat it, or will it eat me?

—LEE K. ABBOTT, "TWENTY QUESTIONS" (1995)

Do you look through

The failures and mistakes and see

Me as the man I want to be?

—ISLA PASCHAL RICHARDSON, "MY DOG AND I" (1946)

What strained and anxious lives dogs must lead, so emotionally
involved in the world of men, whose affections they strive
endlessly to secure, whose authority they are expected
unquestioningly to obey, and whose minds they can never
do more than imperfectly reach and comprehend.

—JOSEPH RANDOLPH ACKERLEY, *MY DOG TULIP* (1956)

I love this little house because
It offers, after dark,
A pause for rest, a rest for paws,
A place to moor my bark.

—ARTHUR GUITERMAN, "MOTTO FOR A DOG HOUSE" (1946)

If killing birds be such a crime,

(Which I can hardly see)

What think you, Sir, of killing Time

With verse address'd to me?

—WILLIAM COWPER,

"ON A SPANIEL, CALLED BEAU, KILLING A YOUNG BIRD" (1793)

Read in the "Dogs' Gazette" that Ll—d G—e is to

tax Pekingese £100 each. Walked to Westminster—

bit Ll—d G—e—tasted like Welsh Rabbit.

—ANONYMOUS, *THE KENNEL* (1910)

My days and nights one equal tenour keep,

Fast but to eat, and only wake to sleep;

Thus stealing along life I live incog,

A very plain and downright honest dog.

—WILLIAM HAMILTON, "INSCRIPTION ON A DOG" (1765)

Their dogs may always be observed at the same time, openly

disparaging the men they keep to one another, and settling where they

shall respectively take their men when they begin to move again.

—ANONYMOUS, *ALL THE YEAR ROUND* (1859)

Every dog should have a man of his own. There is nothing like a well-behaved person around the house to spread the dog's blanket for him, or bring him his supper when he comes home man-tired at night.

—COREY FORD, *EVERY DOG SHOULD HAVE A MAN* (1952)

The argument was very sound . . .
But since the author was a hound,
Its merit went unrecognized.

—JEAN DE LA FONTAINE,
"THE FARMER, THE DOG, AND THE FOX" (1668)

We are going out. You know the pitch of the word,

Probing the tone of thought as it comes through fog

And reaches by devious means

(half-smelt, half-heard)

The four-legged brain of a walk-ecstatic dog.

—HAROLD MONRO, "DOG"

[W]e have the bark of eagerness, as in the chase; that of anger, as well as growling; the yelp or howl of despair, as when shut up; the baying at night; the bark of joy, as when starting on a walk with his master; and the very distinct one of demand or supplication, as when wishing for a door or window to be opened.

—CHARLES DARWIN,
THE DESCENT OF MAN, AND SELECTION IN RELATION TO SEX (1871)

Dogs laugh, but they laugh with their tails.

—MAX EASTMAN (1883-1969), WRITER

When I went over and saw that he wasn't hurt and started laughing at the way he looked, he started laughing too, at least in his own way.
—JOHN GRAVES, *BLUE AND SOME OTHER DOGS* (1981)

[Y]es, Bashan has to laugh too; and as I laugh I marvel at the sight, to me the oddest and most touching thing in the world.
—THOMAS MANN, *BASHAN AND I* (1918)

Were it not for the act of tilting their mugs in mock concentration (usually biting their tongues or the inside of their cheeks as well), they would run the potentially embarrassing risk of laughing—loud, long, uncontrollably—at nearly everything we say to them.
—DANNY SHANAHAN, "HOW TO READ YOUR DOG" (1995)

I've seen a look in dogs' eyes, a quickly vanishing
look of amazed contempt, and I am convinced
that basically dogs think humans are nuts.

—JOHN STEINBECK, *TRAVELS WITH CHARLEY* (1962)

You got to be a hypocrite around a grown woman to get along
with her at all. And then she'll feed you and make a lot of
fuss over you. But the minute you start anything with real
enjoyment in it she's surprised to see you acting that way.

—DON MARQUIS, "BEING A PUBLIC CHARACTER
(AS TOLD BY THE DOG)" (1922)

Ever consider what dogs must think of us? I mean, here we come back from a grocery store with the most amazing haul—chicken, pork, half a cow. They must think we're the greatest hunters on earth!

—ANNE TYLER (B. 1941), NOVELIST AND SHORT STORY WRITER

Remember, never try to be familiar with the person at the end of the broom.

—NOEL DE VIC BEAMISH, *MISS PERFECTION* (1931)

He fought with the he-dogs, and winked at the she-dogs,
A thing that had never been heard of before.
"For the stigma of gluttony, I care not a button!" he
Cried, and ate all he could swallow—and more.

—RUPERT BROOKE, "THE LITTLE DOG'S DAY" (1907)

The media were reporting that I was getting more
publicity than some members of the Cabinet. Considering
some of my press, maybe they should be grateful.

—BARBARA BUSH, *MILLIE'S BOOK* (1990)

Most female dogs decide by the time their pups are weaned that the
whole thing was a terrible mistake, the worst idea they ever had.

—ROGER A. CARAS, *A DOG IS LISTENING* (1992)

Always go out of a room first: get to the door the moment it's opened. You may not get another chance for a long time.

—EDWARD J. M. D. PLUNKETT, LORD DUNSANY,
MY TALKS WITH DEAN SPANLEY (1936)

All this fuss about fleas makes me sick. If you are busy, you don't notice them. If you aren't, they give you something to do.

—JOHN TAINTOR FOOTE, *DUMB-BELL OF BROOKFIELD* (1917)

I rather like a few fleas; they indicate just where one's coat need licking.

—EDWARD J. M. D. PLUNKETT, LORD DUNSANY,
MY TALKS WITH DEAN SPANLEY (1936)

The true philosopher is he who has lost his coat but is free from fleas.

—VIRGINIA WOOLF, *FLUSH* (1933)

Then sooner or later . . . the moon comes over the hill. Of course you can take your own line about that. Personally, I never trusted it. It's the look of it I didn't like, and the sly way it moves. If anything comes by at night I like it to come on footsteps, and I like it to have a smell.

—EDWARD J. M. D. PLUNKETT, LORD DUNSANY,
MY TALKS WITH DEAN SPANLEY (1936)

"Dangers?" he said.

"Yes," I replied.

"The dark of the woods," he answered, "and the mystery of night. There lurked things there of which man himself knew nothing, and even I could only guess."

—EDWARD J. M. D. PLUNKETT, LORD DUNSANY,
MY TALKS WITH DEAN SPANLEY (1936)

Yesterday I was a dog. Today I'm a dog. Tomorrow I'll probably
still be a dog. There's just so little hope of advancement.

—CLARK GESNER, *YOU'RE A GOOD MAN, CHARLIE BROWN* (1967)

Hunting and dog-fighting should be one's main pursuits,
as guarding is a duty, and eating a pastime.

—EDWARD J. M. D. PLUNKETT, LORD DUNSANY,
MY TALKS WITH DEAN SPANLEY (1936)

Most dogs are nice to their masters.

—C. LEONARD FERGUS, *GUN DOG BREEDS* (1992)

Like most dogs that converse with humans he was a thorough
yes type, honoring my every point with agreement.
—JOHN GRAVES, *BLUE AND SOME OTHER DOGS* (1981)

I had always tried . . . to be a friendly kind of a dog
towards boys and humans and dogs, all three.
—DON MARQUIS, "BEING A PUBLIC CHARACTER
(AS TOLD BY THE DOG)" (1922)

We played games. We played King-of-the-Kennel, and
Wolf-at-Bay, and Look-Out-Behind, and Nip-Nip-
Nippy-Legs. Those are all splendid games. . . .
Then we had barking parties. We'd all learned to bark
weeks before, but there is nothing like practice. At barking
parties you try to bark down everyone else. It's glorious!
—JOHN TAINTOR FOOTE, *DUMB-BELL OF BROOKFIELD* (1917)

Instead, I would go out and talk to Jove and he would look
wise and talk back to me, very articulately considering his
limitations, and so we would give each other comfort.

—GERALD HAMMOND, *MAD DOGS AND SCOTSMEN* (1995)

"His champeenship!" And his mouth went wry with scorn.
"Of what? Of a thousand stalls of milk-fed pussyhounds."

—R. G. KIRK, *WHITE MONARCH AND THE GAS-HOUSE PUP* (1917)

i ran so hard i ran so fast
i left the spray behind
i chased the flying flecks of foam
and i outran the wind

an airplane sailing overhead
climbed when it heard me bark
i yelped and leapt right at the sun
until the sky grew dark

some little children on the beach
threw sticks and ran with me
o master let us go again
and play beside the sea

—DON MARQUIS, "PETE AT THE SEASHORE" (1927)

It was necessary, for instance, with no other guide than pain, to learn to calculate the height of objects from the top of which you can jump into space; to convince yourself that it is vain to pursue birds who fly away and that you are unable to clamber up trees after the cats who defy you there; to distinguish between the sunny spots where it is delicious to sleep and the patches of shade in which you shiver; to remark with stupefaction that the rain does not fall inside the houses, that water is cold, uninhabitable and dangerous, while fire is beneficent at a distance, but terrible when you come too near.

—MAURICE MAETERLINCK, *OUR FRIEND, THE DOG* (1904)

Dogs never stand around at parties wondering what to say,
or why they came, or how pitiful they might seem to more
elegant or more amusing or more important guests.

—JEFFREY MOUSSAIEFF MASSON,
DOGS NEVER LIE ABOUT LOVE (1997)

Come in, come in—oh, do come in! This is our house,
but from now on it is yours and everything in it.

—ELIZABETH VON ARNIM, *ALL THE DOGS OF MY LIFE* (1936)

The essence of any game, it seems to me, is to gain possession of
the ball and find a quiet corner where one can destroy it in peace.

—PETER MAYLE, *A DOG'S LIFE* (1995)

Pip has aspirations. In the next turn of the karmic
wheel, he hopes to return as a flamenco dancer: starched
white shirt, black pants, proud castanets.

—DONALD MCCAIG, *EMINENT DOGS, DANGEROUS MEN* (1991)

There's no question about this. I know too well his look of despair and
disapproval when I have just thought that he must be left at home.

—JOHN STEINBECK, *TRAVELS WITH CHARLEY* (1962)

I wonder if other dogs think poodles are
members of a weird religious cult.

—RITA RUDNER (B. 1953), COMEDIAN

THE DOG IN LANGUAGE

Who loves me will love my dog also.

[*Qui me amat, amet et canem meum.*]

—ST. BERNARD (1150)

In my day, male canines were dogs, and females, bitches. That was not a reflection on the bitch's disposition, either. As the language changes, it still calls on canine references for expression. From Old Mother Hubbard fetching her dog's bone to the salty "sea dog," our language is enriched by references to dogs.

There are phrases of doggy origin that have become so familiar as to pass unnoticed—"love me, love my dog," "a-hunting we will go," "beware the dog." Willy-nilly, the dog has entered our language.

He began to bark,

And she began to cry,

"Lawk a mercy on me,

This is none of I!"

—MOTHER GOOSE, "THE OLD WOMAN AND THE PEDLAR" (1806)

"Love me and love my Dog," thou didst reply:

"Love, as both should be lov'd." "I will," said I.

—SIR JOHN HARRINGTON,

"TO HIS WIFE, FOR STRIKING HER DOG" (C. 1600)

"I was the hell of a dog," said the dean.

—EDWARD J. M. D. PLUNKETT, LORD DUNSANY,

MY TALKS WITH DEAN SPANLEY (1936)

No harp like my own could so cheerily play,

And wherever I went was my poor dog Tray.

—THOMAS CAMPBELL, "THE HARPER" (1837)

The cat will mew and dog will have his day.

—WILLIAM SHAKESPEARE, *HAMLET* (1623)

Old Mother Hubbard

Went to the cupboard

To get her poor dog a bone;

But when she came there

The cupboard was bare,

And so the poor dog had none.

—MOTHER GOOSE, "OLD MOTHER HUBBARD" (1805)

I'll get you, my pretty, and your little dog, too.

—NOEL LANGLEY, *THE WIZARD OF OZ* (SCREENPLAY) (1939)

"Who touches a hair of yon gray head
Dies like a dog! March on!" he said.

—JOHN GREENLEAF WHITTIER, "BARBARA FRIETCHIE" [1864]

Then hey for boot and horse, lad,
And round the world away:
Young blood must have its course, lad,
And every dog its day.

—CHARLES KINGSLEY, *THE WATER-BABIES* [1863]

Cry "Havoc" and let slip the dogs of war.

—WILLIAM SHAKESPEARE, *JULIUS CAESAR* (1599)

To hold with the hare and run with the hounds.

—JOHN HEYWOOD (C. 1497-C. 1580), WRITER

The hounds all join the glorious cry,

The huntsman winds his horn,

And a-huntin we will go.

—HENRY FIELDING, "A-HUNTING WE WILL GO" (C. 1745)

Never you mind, the black dog's day has not yet come.
—**PATRICIA DALE-GREEN,** *LORE OF THE DOG* (1967)

●

[T]he contemptible, whining, blind puppy of Atchison. . . .
He can assail no one but in the language of the doggery.
—*KANSAS WEEKLY HERALD* (1855)

●

That isolated case is the editor of the *Iowa Point
Dispatch*—he is half "fyste" and half tumble-bug!! His
quadruped nature is indicated by his bark.
—*WHITE CLOUD KANSAS CHIEF* (1859)

[T]he series of Elizabethan voyagers who had first searched for it, and who offered a national tradition of endurance and sea-doggery.

—FRANCIS SPUFFORD, *I MAY BE SOME TIME* (1996)

I warn them not to come near my door, but beware the dog.

—ARISTOPHANES, *LYSISTRATA* (411 BC)

A hair of the dog that bit us.

—JOHN HEYWOOD, *THE PROVERBS OF JOHN HEYWOOD* (1546)

Or, worse, must I live like a dog, crawling to a master's feet?

—LEW WALLACE, *BEN-HUR* (1880)

Yes—give a dog a bad name and hang him.

—ANTHONY TROLLOPE, *PHINEAS FINN* (1867)

Man is often Dog's severest critic, in spite of his historic protestations of affection and admiration. He calls an unattractive girl a dog, he talks acidly of dogs in the manger, he describes a hard way of life as a dog's life, he observes, cloudily, that this misfortune or that shouldn't happen to a dog, as if most slings and arrows should, and he describes anybody he can't stand as a dirty dog. He notoriously takes the names of the female dog and her male offspring in vain, to denounce blackly members of his own race.

—JAMES THURBER, *THURBER'S DOGS* (1955)

THE FANCY

One day chicken, the next day feathers.

—CONNIE VANACORE, *DOG SHOWING* (1990)

Ah, the world of dog shows—the thrills and chills of showing, handling, judging; the dizzying peaks and valleys of winning and losing; the losing struggle to be fair, to be a good loser, to be a good winner. The boredom, tedium, and solid physical discomfort: crammed under stifling tents in the heat, getting soaked in the rain (shows go on regardless of weather!), eating horrid hot dogs for breakfast, pushing stuck automobiles out of mud, shivering in early-morning, late-fall chills.

And oh! how quickly you become warm and dry and very, very cheerful when you win.

Dog shows were developed to be a showcase for breeding stock.

—GEORGE G. ALSTON, WITH CONNIE VANACORE,
THE WINNING EDGE (1992)

With the exception of Little League baseball, dog shows involve the largest number of amateur participants of any organized sport.

—CONNIE VANACORE, DOG SHOWING (1990)

[W]hen most people think of a dog show, they think of . . . a "conformation show," meaning that the single fundamental quality that makes a winner is bodily perfection.

—JANE AND MICHAEL STERN, DOG EAT DOG (1997)

[T]he Kennel Club, that sine qua non of canine society that
corresponds . . . to the Peerage in the world of our masters.

—G. CORNWALLIS-WEST, *US DOGS* [1938]

[T]he AKC's *Complete Dog Book*. . . . Its 132 breed
histories, each authored by an unidentified expert, are self-
serving, ingenuous, and more often misleading.

—A. HAMILTON ROWAN JR., FOREWORD TO *GUN DOG BREEDS* [1992]

I would love to join the attack on the AKC, but the AKC
isn't the problem, though the fact that it is not the Vatican
is a point which many of its members fail to observe.

—VICKI HEARNE, IN *MONDO CANINE* [1991]

All show dogs have ornamental titles that function as
a code to encourage breed aficionados to remember
the exalted ancestry behind them.
—JANE AND MICHAEL STERN, *DOG EAT DOG* (1997)

Well then what about the judges? You can't
tell me that they are honest.
—FRANK JACKSON, *DIRTY DOG* (1977)

The AKC files may contain information about an applicant.
As a rule, this will be derogatory, since people seldom take
the trouble to write in praise of other exhibitors.

—MAXWELL RIDDLE, "HOW TO BECOME A DOG JUDGE"

Either you know nothing about an Irish Terrier, or, if you do, it was
evident that it was the owner and not the dog, that got the prize.

—DAVID MCLACHAN,
LETTER TO THE *SCOTTISH FANCIER* AND *RURAL GAZETTE* (1887)

Nearly everyone, except perhaps the winning dog's
contingent, is convinced that the judge is blind, ignorant,
on the take, or has a personal vendetta against them.

—JANE AND MICHAEL STERN, *DOG EAT DOG* (1997)

I have known a man act as a judge of foxterriers who had never bred
one in his life, had never seen a fox in front of hounds, had never seen
a terrier go to ground, . . . had not even seen a terrier chase a rabbit.

—RAWDON BRIGGS LEE,
*A HISTORY AND DESCRIPTION OF THE MODERN DOGS
OF GREAT BRITAIN AND IRELAND* (1903)

There is often talk at ringside about the competence,
honesty and even the birthright of some judges.

—CONNIE VANACORE, *DOG SHOWING* (1990)

Who the man with the white waistcoat was who offered
a bribe of a fiver to one of the judges at Cruft's?

—ANONYMOUS, *THE BRITISH FANCIER* (1892)

Well, there are politics in everything in life, and that is
a fact that the owner-handler has to recognize.

—GEORGE G. ALSTON, WITH CONNIE VANACORE,
THE WINNING EDGE (1992)

It is part of the dog breeders' lives that they must suddenly accept the mantle of greatness when they take top prize in a show that they have declared atrocious and from a judge they have deemed cockeyed.

—JANE AND MICHAEL STERN, *DOG EAT DOG* (1997)

Exhibitors have to reckon with many kinds of judges. . . . The weak-
minded, well-meaning man, who never can make up his mind and
gets hot and flustered and nervous, and makes the exhibitors cross and
takes all the life out of the exhibits by having them lifted up and down
and sent round and round the ring fifty times where once would suffice.
. . . The rare judge, who knows his business, who is firm, courteous,
and dignified in the ring, and punctual in getting there, who is rapid
and decided in his awards, and perfectly consistent and reliable.

—JUDITH ANNE BLUNT-LYTTON, BARONESS WENTWORTH,
TOY DOGS AND THEIR ANCESTORS (1911)

When he has completed the questionnaires the applicant has
to swear that he has received no help from established judges
in answering the questions. It can be presumed that those who
cheat on this will not be particularly honorable judges.

—MAXWELL RIDDLE, "HOW TO BECOME A DOG JUDGE"

Oh, you'd be surprised, sir, at the way all the big dog
fanciers swindle their customers over pedigrees.
—JARASLOV HAŠEK, *THE GOOD SOLDIER ŠVEJK* (1921)

Should the cross nick, however, spare no pains to continue
it, if circumstances will enable you to do so—that is to say, if
the dog and the bitch are within 500 miles of each other.
—CHARLES J. APPERLEY (NIMROD), *LIFE OF A SPORTSMAN* (1842)

On the other hand, you can obtain some very pleasing results indeed
by forgetting to close the right door at the right time if you own
the sort of terrier that the Kennel Club wouldn't look at and your
neighbour is the proud owner of a pedigree show-winning dog.

—JOHN TICKNER, *TICKNER'S TERRIERS* (1977)

The show-ring is the death-knell of usefulness for
all animals; I need only mention the show hunter,
the carrier-pigeon, and the show greyhound.

—CAPTAIN LAWRENCE FITZ-BARNARD, *FIGHTING SPORTS* (1921)

Given man's delight in inventing games, and then elevating them
to such a status that national prestige depends upon them, it is
likely that competitions involving dogs go back a very long way.

—FRANK JACKSON, "IN COMPETITION"

Speaking out of the depths of native ignorance,
I assert that the extremely high-bred dogs of the
bench show were the ugliest of their kind.

—SHIRLEY DARE, *SPIRIT OF THE TIMES* (1877)

You don't win any dog shows staying home.

—MILDRED NICOLL (1930-2006),
PROFESSIONAL HANDLER AND JUDGE

There is an old axiom, "An exhibitor's business is to hide his dog's faults and a judge's to find them."

—A. G. STURGEON, *BULLDOGDOM* (1920)

If you do not believe that your dog is a precious commodity, get a different attitude, or a different dog.

—GEORGE G. ALSTON, WITH CONNIE VANACORE, *THE WINNING EDGE* (1992)

If you are of a temperament that cannot accept losses, perhaps you are in the wrong sport. . . . A loss is not the end of the world. It is only the end of the day.

—CONNIE VANACORE, *DOG SHOWING* (1990)

If an exhibitor cannot both win and lose decently, his place is at home.

—A. G. STURGEON, *BULLDOGDOM* (1920)

The "sour grapes" syndrome is alive and well in dogdom.

—CONNIE VANACORE, *DOG SHOWING* (1990)

I'm surprised that you show dogs though, I
mean it's an odd sort of hobby.

—FRANK JACKSON, *DIRTY DOG* (1977)

Like golf, dog shows are a gentleman's sport.

—ROBERT AND JANE FORSYTH,
THE FORSYTH GUIDE TO SUCCESSFUL DOG SHOWING (1975)

The operative word in dog showing is "sport." It is the "sport of dogs," a phrase that sometimes seems to get lost in the heat of competition or the desire to own a top-winning specimen.

—CONNIE VANACORE, *DOG SHOWING* (1990)

The only other function comparable to it in length of time, solemnity, and absence of all spiritual or physical compensations is the pibroch playing at a Highland gathering.

—FREDERICK WATSON, *HUNTING PIE* (1931)

A dog has to think shows are more fun than sitting on the couch, drinking a beer and watching the ball game.

—GEORGE G. ALSTON, WITH CONNIE VANACORE,
THE WINNING EDGE (1992)

All night long they talked and sang, and passed greetings
with old pals, and the homesick puppies howled dismal.
Them that couldn't sleep wouldn't let no others sleep, and
all the electric lights burned in the roof, and in my eyes.

—RICHARD HARDING DAVIS, *THE BAR SINISTER* (1903)

Show dogs and their handlers remind me of Brooke
Shields and her mother: an incredibly disheveled person
tethered to an impeccably groomed animal.

—MARGO KAUFMAN (1953-2000), HUMORIST

You may think that professional handlers are lazy because they
stand outside the ring, telling dirty jokes, watching girls in
short dresses or guys in tight pants in the ring next to theirs.

—GEORGE G. ALSTON, WITH CONNIE VANACORE,
THE WINNING EDGE (1992)

Showing dogs is the only sport that, by the payment
of an entry fee and with no training whatsoever, you
can compete directly with a professional.

—GEORGE G. ALSTON, WITH CONNIE VANACORE,
THE WINNING EDGE (1992)

It is bad form to stare at the judge.

—ROBERT AND JANE FORSYTH,

THE FORSYTH GUIDE TO SUCCESSFUL DOG SHOWING (1975)

The perfect handler is invisible.

—GEORGE G. ALSTON, WITH CONNIE VANACORE,

THE WINNING EDGE (1992)

[B]arking at every dog as he come in; daring him to fight, and ordering him out, and asking him what breed of dog he thought he was, anyway.

—RICHARD HARDING DAVIS, *THE BAR SINISTER* (1903)

[T]he toy group which consisted of one dog because a snow storm resulted in 1,200 absentees, leaving only 70 dogs in competition.

—AKC JUDGES' NEWSLETTER

Personally, I trust it will never be a usual thing for a lady to judge large classes at our leading shows.

—SIDNEY H. DEACON, *SHOW BULLDOGS* (1904)

Putting up good dogs is easy. Finding them is often well nigh unto impossible.

—DENNY KODNER (1924-2010), HANDLER AND BREEDER

THE BREEDS

Border collies are bred to do exacting work at great distances from their handler. They are intelligent, obsessive, and physically powerful. Their handler needs both savvy and grit.

—DONALD MCCAIG, *NOP'S HOPE* (1994)

Each of those two hundred breeds the AKC registers has a breed standard—how they should look and move and behave in the show ring. What's not covered is the essence of the breed—the brains (or lack thereof), personality, and fetishes that each breed representative has. But proud (or dismayed) owners of various breeds have set down the particular charms of their obsession, and I have quoted them.

A particular dog's breeding, then, can imbue it with a
strong sense of functions and a set of specific behavioral
patterns in addition to a specific coat or eye color.

—MYRNA MILANI, D.V.M., *DOG SMART* (1997)

It is important to know not only a breed's country
of origin, but also the characteristics of the people
who developed and nurtured the breed.

—EDD BIVIN, *AKC GAZETTE* (MARCH 1996)

The first rule for picking a pup: Don't ever look
to pup to pick a pup. Look to parents.

—BILL TARRANT, *THE BEST WAY TO TRAIN YOUR GUN DOG* (1977)

On Alaskan Malamutes

My principal religious belief is a conviction that the
Alaskan malamute is the stairway to heaven.
—SUSAN CONANT, *TRUE CONFESSIONS* (1995)

Malamutes, some of them, can sleep like nothing else
that's animate. Convinced that there is nothing on earth
that wants to hurt them, they can drop off in the middle
of noise and crowds and sleep like cinder blocks.
—DANIEL PINKWATER, "ARNOLD COMES HOME" (2014)

Their brain [is] like a piece of river rock.
—PETER JENNINGS (1938-2005), JOURNALIST

On Beagles

They are the smallest of the hound race used in this
country, are exquisite in their scent of the hare, and
indefatigably vigilant in the pursuit of her.

—WILLIAM TAPLIN, *THE SPORTSMAN'S CABINET* (1803)

To plains with well-breath'd beagles we repair,
And trace the mazes of the circling hare;
(Beasts, urged by us, their fellow beast pursue,
And learn of man each other to undo.)

—ALEXANDER POPE, "WINDSOR·FOREST" (1713)

On Border Collies

Border Collies are very bright, quick, and more than a little weird.

—DONALD McCAIG, *NOP'S TRIALS* (1994)

Indeed, in some circles the Border collie is called the eye dog. Their eyes, like a carpenter's hammer, are the tools of the trade. They use them, like a preacher's sermon, to show their flock the way.

—ARTHUR YORINKS, *THE EYES HAVE IT* (1995)

He was a gash an' faithfu' tyke,
As ever lap a sheugh or dyke,
His honest, sonsie, baws'nt face
Aye gat him friends in ilka place.

—ROBERT BURNS, "THE TWA DOGS" (1786)

On Boxers

Today the boxer
Is fashionable and snappy;
But I never saw a boxer
Who looked thoroughly happy.

—E. B. WHITE, "FASHIONS IN DOGS" (1936)

On Bull Terriers

He had sleepy pink eyes and thin pink lips, and he was as white all over as his own white teeth, and under his white skin you could see his muscles, hard and smooth, like the links of a steel chain.

—RICHARD HARDING DAVIS, *THE BAR SINISTER* [1903]

You didn't have to throw a stick into the water to get him to go in. Of course, he would bring back a stick if you did throw one in. He would have brought back a piano if you had thrown one in.

—JAMES THURBER, "SNAPSHOT OF A DOG" [1935]

[R]olling in his run, and smiling as bull terriers will.

—RUDYARD KIPLING, "GARM-A HOSTAGE" [1899]

On Chow Chows

They were my first encounter with the beautiful uselessness that feeds the soul, the nonstop obstinacies that lie at the heart of love and of art.

—ENID SHOMER, "MR. AND MRS. FOO" [1995]

On Crossbreeds

Crossing undoubtedly adds to the dog's intelligence. The
highest-bred dogs are, as a rule, wanting in this faculty.

—THOMAS PEARCE (IDSTONE),
THE DOG, WITH SIMPLE DIRECTIONS FOR HIS TREATMENT (1872)

Mongrels are always smartest.

—RUDYARD KIPLING, "A SEA DOG" (1930)

As to colour, a dog ought not to be red or black or white altogether; a
uniform colour is not a sign of breeding but rather of a common animal.

—XENOPHON, *CYNEGETICUS* (C. FOURTH CENTURY BC)

My father was a St. Bernard, my mother was a Collie,
but I am a Presbyterian. This is what my mother told
me; I do not know these nice distinctions myself.

—MARK TWAIN, "A DOG'S TALE" (1903)

I like a bit of mongrel myself, whether it's a man
or a dog; they're the best for every day.

—GEORGE BERNARD SHAW, *MISALLIANCE* (1910)

[T]he shorter the pedigree the better the dog, and now if I could
get them I should like to keep dogs that never had a father.

—H. C. BARKLEY,
*STUDIES IN THE ART OF RAT-CATCHING, FOR
THE USE OF SCHOOLS* (1896)

On Dachshunds

A Dachshund sniffing round a tree
Made such a wondrous bend, sir,
He filled himself with mystery—
Not knowing his own end, sir.

—JOHN E. DONOVAN, "THE DACHSHUND" (1946)

Dachshunds are ideal dogs for small children, as they are
already stretched and pulled to such a length that the
child cannot do much harm one way or the other.

—ROBERT BENCHLEY (1889-1945), HUMORIST

On Doberman Pinschers

All Dobermans should be named "Einstein." Well, perhaps
that's too lavish praise. They're a bit weak on mathematics,
but they certainly could earn a Ph.D. in any other subject.

—**MORTON WILSON, DOG TRAINER**

On English Bulldogs

Who needs twice-a-day, eyes-closed, inward voyages when you
can slip into oblivion by becoming one with a sixty-pound teddy
bear of a mantra who looks like a canine Popeye (mammoth
biceps and pectorals followed by a bell-jar waist), understands your
every mood shift and has as many of his own, and participates in a
mystical fusion with subhuman (or is it superhuman) sensations?

—**ROBERT ROSENBLUM, "TRUE ROMANCE" (1995)**

[T]hat certain uptilt of chin and backroll of eyes which have
been patented for buldoggy use the wide world over.

—R. G. KIRK, *WHITE MONARCH AND THE GAS-HOUSE PUP* [1917]

Pelléas had a great bulging powerful forehead, like that of Socrates
or Verlaine; and, under a little black nose, blunt as a churlish assent,
a pair of large hanging and symmetrical chops, which made his head
a sort of massive obstinate, pensive and three-cornered menace.

—MAURICE MAETERLINCK, *OUR FRIEND, THE DOG* [1904]

[T]his low, squat, canine battleship.

—R. G. KIRK, *WHITE MONARCH AND THE GAS-HOUSE PUP* [1917]

[T]hat stiff-legged swashbuckling roll and captivating swagger
which makes his breed win into human hearts at a glance.

—R. G. KIRK, *WHITE MONARCH AND THE GAS-HOUSE PUP* [1917]

On Field Dogs

A good springer will hunt any sort of fowl in any type of cover.

—C. LEONARD FERGUS, *GUN DOG BREEDS* (1992)

[C]ockers of working strains. They are quick and cheerful dogs with excellent noses, though sometimes headstrong, and their small size, although a handicap when it comes to retrieving a hare or a goose, lets them penetrate deeper into tight cover than larger dogs.

—GERALD HAMMOND, *THE CURSE OF THE COCKERS* (1993)

When he hath found the bird, he keepeth sure and fast silence, he stayeth his steps and will proceed no further and with a close, covert, watching eye, layeth his belly to the ground.

—JOHN CAIUS [ON ENGLISH SETTERS], *OF ENGLISHE DOGGES* (1576)

[A]s with all breeds, they require a consistent, vigilant trainer.

—C. LEONARD FERGUS [ON SPRINGERS], *GUN DOG BREEDS* [1992]

[I]n variety of color and elegance of clothing no animal
of his species will at all bear comparison with him.

—J. W. CARLETON [CRAVEN] [ON ENGLISH SETTERS],
THE YOUNG SPORTSMAN'S MANUAL [1849]

Field spaniel owners report that their dogs are prodigious snorers.
—C. LEONARD FERGUS, *GUN DOG BREEDS* (1992)

The souls of deceased bailiffs and common constables
are in the bodies of setting dogs and pointers. . . . There
are also a set of sad dogs derived from attornies.
—WILLIAM TAPLIN, *THE SPORTSMAN'S CABINET* (1803)

They're so dumb that they get lost on the end of their leash.
—MICHAEL FOX [ON IRISH SETTERS] (B. 1937), VETERINARIAN

English Setters mature earlier, but have about
ten shows in them before they quit.
—GEORGE G. ALSTON, WITH CONNIE VANACORE,
THE WINNING EDGE (1992)

See how the well-taught pointer leads the way.
—JOHN GAY, "RURAL SPORTS" (1713)

Brittanys were bred as poacher's dogs. . . . They were an extension of
the old rogue's arm, trained to look innocent and unprepossessing,
all the time plotting, thinking, scheming to make game.

—JOEL M. VANCE (1934-2020), WRITER

He struck me as being slightly rude in his stand-offish
way, but obviously a person to know, to admire, and,
later on, to like. That applies to all Chesapeakes.

—J. WENTWORTH DAY, *THE DOG IN SPORT* (1938)

The show-bench and the drawing-room have made fools of them,
undermined their character, ruined their stamina, set their nerves
on edge. . . . I doubt if you could ever do that with a Chesapeake.
He will probably bite someone finally, just as a protect, and then
walk out of the house, a dog in search of a man for a master.

—J. WENTWORTH DAY, *THE DOG IN SPORT* (1938)

Boy has a nose like the muzzle of a double-barrel shotgun
and he can rest his chin on the table and pull a slice of
bread toward him from a foot away, two inches at a sniff.
And he can strike with the speed of a rattlesnake.

—SPARSE GREY HACKLE [ON GERMAN SHORTHAIRED
POINTERS], *AN HONEST ANGLER* (1998)

On Golden Retrievers

[Y]ou have to envy her, because she is never without a purpose in life, never bored, never unsure of herself as long as there is a tennis ball, or a golf ball, or an apple, or a snowball, or even a basketball somewhere around, because if she can't pick it up, at least she can roll it.

—JANE SMILEY, "FETCH" (1995)

The delightful story that had the "six circus-performing Russian Trackers" as antecedents for the Golden Retriever is only that—a story— . . . which has no basis in fact.

—*THE COMPLETE DOG BOOK*, OFFICIAL PUBLICATION OF THE AMERICAN KENNEL CLUB (1977)

Retrievers just naturally love humans—
and, just as naturally, we respond.

—C. LEONARD FERGUS, *GUN DOG BREEDS* (1992)

On Great Danes

Great Danes are above tricks and resolute about the irrelevance of swimming to the life of an intelligent canine.

—JANE SMILEY, "FETCH" (1995)

Things that upset a terrier may pass virtually
unnoticed by a Great Dane.

—SMILEY BLANTON (1882-1966), PSYCHIATRIST

Why not have a Danish dog? I know of one as big as a camel-
leopard, by Jove. It would almost pull your brougham.

—WILLIAM MAKEPEACE THACKERAY, *VANITY FAIR* (1848)

A Great Dane is not unlike your average human, a generalist
who over the centuries has been taught to engage in
various activities, from guarding to killing wild boar to
cleaning up the scraps under medieval banquet tables.

—JANE SMILEY, "FETCH" (1995)

On Greyhounds

Seest thou the gaze-hound!
how, with glance severe,
From the close herd he marks the destin'd deer;
How ev'ry nerve the greyhound's stretch displays.

—THOMAS TICKELL, "HUNTING"

Despite the commotion, the greyhounds are silent. They
are not given to the inelegant task of barking.

—SUSAN OLASKY, *A DOG'S LIFE: RACERS TURNED PETS* (1996)

A greyhounde should be headed lyke a snake,

And neckyd lyke a drake,

Fotyd like a cat,

Tayled lyke a ratte,

Syded lyke a teme,

And chyned lyke a bream.

—JULIANA BERNERS, "THE PROPERTIES OF A GOOD GREYHOUNDE"

Though most greyhound owners brag about the breed's

intelligence, the dogs are not suited for every task.

—SUSAN OLASKY, *A DOG'S LIFE: RACERS TURNED PETS* (1996)

On Hounds

My hounds are bred out of the Spartan kind,

So flew'd, so sanded: and their heads are hung

With ears that sweep away the morning dew;

Crook-knee'd, and dewlapp'd like Thessalian bulls;

Slow in pursuit, but match'd in mouth like bells,

Each under each. A cry more tuneable

Was never holla'd to, nor cheer'd with horn,

In Crete, in Sparta, nor in Thessaly:

Judge when you hear.

—WILLIAM SHAKESPEARE, *A MIDSUMMER NIGHT'S DREAM* (1605)

What attracts the dog lover is not the doggishness of a dog . . . but its human qualities—faithfulness, gratitude, patience in waiting for its master. . . . No human being has such an entreating expression as a basset hound, no human being is as loyal as his dog.

—MIDAS DEKKERS, *DEAREST PET* (1994)

It seems to me, however, that legend and lore are more likely than early breeders and fanciers to have given the bloodhound his name. In any case, it has always had a fearsome sound to the ignorant ear, and one of the gentlest of all species, probably, indeed, the gentlest, has been more maligned through the centuries than any other great Englishman with the exception of King Richard the Third.

—JAMES THURBER, *THURBER'S DOGS* (1955)

The hounds . . . were of the orthodox three colours, black, white and tan, with the long hanging ears (that irresistibly suggest the portraits of Mrs. Barrett Browning) and beautiful romantic eyes, and pointed tan toes, that again suggest the poetess, and would look charming in black satin sandals.

—EDITH SOMERVILLE,
"AN APPRECIATION," IN *THE SILVER HORN* (1934)

Two dogs of black Saint Hubert's breed
Unmatch'd for courage, breath, and speed,
Fast on his flying traces came.

—SIR WALTER SCOTT, "THE LADY OF THE LAKE" (1810)

Their manners were to come when called,
Their flesh was sinew knit to bone,
Their courage like a banner blown.

—JOHN MASEFIELD,
REYNARD THE FOX, OR THE GHOST HEATH RUN (1919)

On Irish Setters

Shamus has a welcome song,
Also a welcome dance:
He performs for all newcomers
With a cavalierly prance.

—CAMPASPE, "TO AN IRISH SETTER PUP" (1946)

On Irish Wolfhounds

All seven of my Irish [wolfhound] friends possessed a consciousness—
awareness of self, awareness of selflessness, awareness of mortality—
far more persuasive than that of many people I have known.

—EDWARD ALBEE, "HARRY SIGHING" (1995)

Long and grey and gaunt he lies,
A Lincoln among dogs.

**—CHRISTOPHER MORLEY,
"AT THE DOG SHOW: TO AN IRISH WOLFHOUND" (1917)**

[H]e guessed that from their rolling, leaping gait—gracefully fast, like cheetahs or antelopes—that these were Irish wolfhounds, the coyote hunters of his youth. . . . [H]e remembered the wolfhounds' vaguely terrifying size, their power and lithesome restlessness, and it seemed to him in the desert now that these shadowy creatures spilling through the night had just that sort of galloping height, that equine size and speed.

—DAVID GUTERSON, *EAST OF THE MOUNTAINS* (1998)

Their deeply friendly nature expresses itself in great, swathing tail wags that can clear a table of bibelots in a second—a perfect argument against bibelots, of course.

—EDWARD ALBEE, "HARRY SIGHING" (1995)

On Labrador Retrievers

[H]e had confidence in the future. He knew the good times
would come again some day. Meanwhile, he was prepared
to wait with the patience peculiar to Labradors.

—GERALD HAMMOND, *MAD DOGS AND SCOTSMEN* (1995)

Labradors [make] lousy watchdogs. They usually bark when
there is a stranger about, but it is an expression of unmitigated
joy at the chance to meet somebody new, not a warning.

—NORMAN STRUNG (1941-1991), EDITOR

Labradors are entirely gut-oriented.

—GERALD HAMMOND, *MAD DOGS AND SCOTSMEN* (1995)

The real breed may be known by its close coat which turns
the water off like oil, and, above all, a tail like an otter.

—EARL OF MALMESBURY IN 1887

I always find it endearing when a Labrador, that most
mature and dignified of breeds on the surface, reveals
the puppyishness which is never far beneath.

—GERALD HAMMOND, *MAD DOGS AND SCOTSMEN* (1995)

On Mastiffs

The "mastive or bandogge" was described . . . as "vast,
huge, stubborn, eager, of a heavy and burdensome body,
and therefore but of little swiftness" and it "took fast
hold with its teeth and held on beyond all credit."

—HENRY DAVIS, QUOTING ABRAHAM FLEMING, *THE DOG AS GUARD*

●

[H]is disposition must neither be too gentle, nor too curst, that
he neither faune upon a theefe nor flee upon his friends; very
waking; no gadder abroad, nor lavish of his mouth, barking without
cause; neither maketh it any matter though he be not swifte, for
he is but to fight at home, and to give warning of the enemie.

—BARNABE GOOGE'S TRANSLATION OF CONRAD
HERESBACH, *THE BANDOG FOR THE HOUSE* (1577)

●

[T]he ancient mastiff brindle that had come to be a
color dreaded by the bare-calved legions of Rome.

—R. G. KIRK, *WHITE MONARCH AND THE GAS-HOUSE PUP* (1917)

●

A mastiff, of true English blood,
Loved fighting better than his food.

—JOHN GAY, "THE MASTIFFS" (1727)

On Newfoundlands

Newfoundland dogs are good to save children from drowning,
but you must have a pond of water handy and a child, or else
there will be no profit in boarding a Newfoundland.

—JOSH BILLINGS, *ESSAYS* (1880)

On Poodles

Poodles always listen attentively while being scolded,
looking innocent, bewildered and misunderstood.

—JAMES THURBER, *LANTERNS AND LANCES* [1961]

For when Charley is groomed and clipped and washed he
is as pleased with himself as is a man with a good tailor
or a woman newly patinaed by a beauty parlor, all of
whom can believe they are like that clear through.

—JOHN STEINBECK, *TRAVELS WITH CHARLEY* [1962]

FAUST: Look close! What do you take the beast to be?
WAGNER: A poodle, searching with his natural bent
And snuffing for his master's scent.

—JOHANN WOLFGANG VON GOETHE, *FAUST* [1808]

On Sheepdogs

The Dogge that is for the folde must neyther be so gaunt nor swyft
as the Greyhound, nor so fatte nor heavy as the Masty of the
house, but very strong, and able to fight and followe the chase,
that he may be able to beate away the Woolfe or other beastes.

—BARNABE GOOGE'S TRANSLATION OF CONRAD
HERESBACH, *FOURE BOOKES OF HUSBANDRIE* (1577)

Bear, our first Old English sheep dog, wasn't our
dog. Despite his superiority in hearing, smelling,
and growing hair, he was one of us people.

—ROBERT CANZONERI,
"BEAR, BULL, BUBBA, AND OTHER FOLK" (1995)

On Saint Bernards

St. Bernard, whose small intellect is what might be expected of a
race living on the top of a mountain with only monks for company.

—CHARLES DICKENS, *ALL THE YEAR ROUND* **(1859–1895)**

Champion Plinlimmon Jr [St. Bernard] . . . was very heavy as a
corpse, weighing on the morning of his death one hundred and ninety
pounds and one-half. It took five able-bodied men to remove him.

—GUSTAVE FOX, *THE AMERICAN FIELD* **(1894)**

On Terriers

For your Pollicle Dog is a dour Yorkshire tyke,
And his braw Scottish cousins are snappers and biters,
And every dog-jack of them notable fighters;
And so they stepped out, with their pipers in order,
Playing *When the Blue Bonnets Came Over the Border*.

—T. S. ELIOT, "OF THE AWEFULL BATTLE OF
THE PEKES AND THE POLLICLES" (1939)

Most terriers are independent, tough dogs, with a predisposition to
bark when they get excited (and they get excited very easily).

—STANLEY COREN, *THE INTELLIGENCE OF DOGS* (1994)

Aberdeen terriers are intelligent . . . but so austere and full
of the Calvinistic spirit that it is impossible for an ordinary
erring human being not to feel ill at ease in their presence.

—P. G. WODEHOUSE (1881-1975), WRITER

[A]n Airedale's desire for complete possession of one
human. . . . We simply must own someone.

—NOEL DE VIC BEAMISH, *MISS PERFECTION* [1931]

Let Terriers small be bred, and taught to bay,
When Foxes find unstopt Badjers earthe.

—ANONYMOUS, RECORDS OF THE OLD CHARLTON
HUNT BY THE EARL OF MARCH [1737]

Outspeak the Squire, "Give room, I pray,
And hie the terriers in;
The warriors of the fight are they,
And every fight they win."

—ANONYMOUS, "RING-OUZEL"

[T]hey are so exceedingly sturdy that it is proverbial that the
only thing fatal to them is being run over by an automobile—in
which case the car itself knows that it has been in a fight.

—DOROTHY PARKER [ON SCOTTISH TERRIERS],
"TOWARD THE DOG DAYS" (1928)

[O]ne of the most popular is undoubtedly the fox-terrier.
This is assuredly the doggiest dog we possess, the most
aggressive, born to trouble as the sparks fly upward.

—W. H. HUDSON, *THE BOOK OF A NATURALIST* (1919)

An Airedale, erect beside the chauffeur of a Rolls-Royce,
Often gives you the impression he's there from choice.

—E. B. WHITE, "FASHIONS IN DOGS" (1936)

Terriers are quite convinced that all terriers are not only
beautiful but are the most expert of all because they know
that to get the best out of Man they must not only be kind
but also be firm and therefore handle Man with a very firm
paw indeed—the little steel paw in the little velvet glove and
sometimes with the help of the little steel teeth as well.

—JOHN TICKNER, *TICKNER'S TERRIERS* (1977)

Fox-terriers are born with about four times as much original sin in them as other dogs are, and it will take years and years of patient effort on the part of us Christians to bring about any appreciable reformation in the rowdiness of the fox-terrier nature.

—JEROME K. JEROME, *THREE MEN IN A BOAT* (1889)

My Christmas will be a whole lot wetter and merrier
If somebody sends me a six-weeks-old Boston terrier.

—E. B. WHITE, "FASHIONS IN DOGS" (1936)

It [the Boston terrier] is a flat-faced, bug-eyed, wheezing, snorting, snoring, flatulent little excrescence almost always delivered by Caesarian section because of its ugly, outsize knob of a head.

—DANIEL PINKWATER,
"WHEN I SAID I WANTED A DOG, BOOTSIE WAS
NOT WHAT I HAD IN MIND" (1995)

An Airedale can do anything any other dog can do
and then whip the other dog if he has to.

—THEODORE ROOSEVELT (1858-1919), US PRESIDENT

[The Skye terrier] was brought out of barbarous borders from
the uttermost contryes northward, . . . which, by reason of the
length of heare, makes showe neither of face nor body.

—JOHN CAIUS, *OF ENGLISHE DOGGES* (1576)

Bull terriers and fox terriers however are noteworthy for their roaming
and homing instincts and, not being highly nervous dogs, are quite
at home when traveling by train or other public conveyance.

—ALBERT H. TRAPMAN,
A DOG LOOKS FOR HIS MASTER BY TRAIN (1928)

On Toys

You don't sweat to struggle free,

Work in rags and rotting breeches.

Puppy, have a laugh at me,

Digging in the ditches.

—LOUIS UNTERMEYER,

"LINES TO A POMERANIAN PUPPY VALUED AT 3,500 DOLLARS" (1917)

Many people, I know, disparage Pekes, but take it
from me, they are all right. If they have a fault, it is
a tendency to think too much of themselves.

—P. G. WODEHOUSE (1881-1975), WRITER

The dog's tail and ears have been sent downstairs to be
washed; from which circumstances we infer that the animal
is no more. His forelegs have been delivered to the boots
to be brushed, which strengthens the supposition.

—CHARLES DICKENS [ON A PUG], *SKETCHES BY BOZ* [1836]

Let the Lion Dog be small; let it wear the swelling
cape of dignity around its neck; let it display the
billowing standard of pomp above its back.

—DOWAGER EMPRESS CIXI [ON PEKINGESE], "PEARLS OF WISDOM"

On Various Breeds

The Pharaoh hound is the only breed of dog that blushes—
or needs to: Pharaoh hounds have filthy minds.

—HOWARD OGDEN, *PENSAMENTOES*

It looks like a miniature hippopotamus with
badly fitting panty hose all over.

—ROGER A. CARAS [ON SHAR-PEIS],
A CELEBRATION OF DOGS [1982]

We are glad you have a Dalmatian. They are much more
sensible than any other breed of dog I know—and I've known
many breeds. . . . Dalmatians are not only superior to other
dogs, they are like all dogs, infinitely less stupid than men.

—EUGENE O'NEILL [1888-1953], PLAYWRIGHT, IN A LETTER

Let me tell you about the Bullmastiff. . . . This

is a very special breed, a breed apart.

This is a breed with dignity, this is a dog that suffers in silence.

This is a breed that cannot be taken for a joke.

This is a dog with a neck that starts at thirty inches.

This is a dog that can break your spine.

This is a dog that must be loved!

This is a dog who is one of the greatest psychiatrists going.

You look in his face and you forget everything.

—VITO ANCONA (1948-2024), BULLMASTIFF FANCIER

●

As hound and greyhounds, mongrels, spaniels, curs,

Shoughs, water-rugs, and demi-wolves are cleipt

All by the name of dogs.

—WILLIAM SHAKESPEARE, *THE TRAGEDIE OF MACBETH* (1623)

●

They are not good indoor dogs. They like to chew things—furniture

and wood. I left one outside and it chewed the bumpers off my Toyota.

—DR. ANTONIO GALLARDO (B. 1948), PRESA CANARIO FANCIER

And a Few New Breeds

Pointer + Setter =
Poinsetter, a traditional Christmas pet

Great Pyrenees + Dachshund =
Pyradachs, a puzzling breed

Pekingese + Lhasa Apso =
Peekasso, an abstract dog

Labrador Retriever + Curly Coated Retriever =
Lab Coat Retriever, the choice of research scientists

Newfoundland + Basset Hound =
Newfound Asset Hound, a dog for financial advisors

Malamute + Pointer =
Moot Point, owned by . . . oh, well, it doesn't matter anyway

TRAINING

There's only one way you can be a dog man. You must be God.

Only God gives and takes, favors and denies, pleasures and pains.

If you've no mind to be God, then you've no mind to have a dog.

—BILL TARRANT, *THE BEST WAY TO TRAIN YOUR GUN DOG* (1977)

Dogs' approach to training is as widely varied as the way they look. It's all part of that breed personality function—the genes that make working dogs responsive and easy to teach and make terriers difficult to convince. Manuals on training have been produced since the early printing press, I believe, and still dogs drag their owners down the street, nip the sheep's heels, flush the birds, and misbehave on the carpet. Training is good but not always successful.

These quotations reflect the writers' observations on training—or the lack thereof.

First you learn a new language, profanity; and second you
learn not to discipline your dogs when you're mad, and
that's most of the time when you're training dogs.
—LOU SCHULTZ, IN *365 DOGS CALENDAR* (1991)

[M]ost of the dogs in the nonsporting, terrier, and hound groups
. . . are noted for their reluctance to acknowledge authority.
—BETTY FISHER AND SUZANNE DELZIO,
SO YOUR DOG'S NOT LASSIE (1998)

An extraordinary number of failures at formal tracking trials happen
when the handler pulls the dog away from the trail, which may be
one of the reasons the bigger, stronger dogs do so well at tracking.
—VICKI HEARNE, *ADAM'S TASK* (1986)

Some day, if I ever get a chance, I shall write a book or
warning on the character and temperament of the dachshund
and why he can't be trained and shouldn't be. I would
rather train a striped zebra to balance an Indian club than
induce a dachshund to heed my slightest command.

—E. B. WHITE (1899-1985), WRITER

I like to think that the training is taking place in the head,
not the stomach. A kind word in his ear is making the brain
work, food in the stomach only makes the bowels work.

—RICHARD A. WOLTERS, *GUN DOG* (1961)

Now a dog that can't, after three years of yard training, learn
the meanings of the words "come," "whoa," and "heel" will
learn, after one trip to the pooch health parlor, not only
what the word "vet" means, but he will learn to spell it as in:
"Catch the dog because I'm taking him to the v-e-t." After this
statement, Sport vanishes like snowflakes in a campfire.

—STEVE SMITH, *THE VET*

Pull (n or v): An equal and opposite force perpetrated
on both ends of a leash that results in the inevitable
tripping and falling of the human involved.

—BETTY FISHER AND SUZANNE DELZIO,
***SO YOUR DOG'S NOT LASSIE* (1998)**

My husband and I have worked out a system to get the dogs
to do what he wants: He tells me, and I tell the dog.

—SUSAN CONANT, *TRUE CONFESSIONS* [1995]

He did real good. He listens to his trainer real good. He just
don't listen to me. I still can't get him to do nothin'.

—EVANDER HOLYFIELD [B. 1962], HEAVYWEIGHT BOXER

When I get a new dog I never ask who he is, or who his
father was, but I go by his looks and his performance.

—H. C. BARKLEY,
*STUDIES IN THE ART OF RAT-CATCHING, FOR
THE USE OF SCHOOLS* [1896]

I like them all—pointers, setters, retrievers, spaniels—
what have you. I've had good ones and bad of several kinds.
Most of the bad ones were my fault and most of the good
ones would have been good under any circumstances.

—GENE HILL [1928-1997], AUTHOR

I arrived at my adult years with a fairly intact urban, middle-class, sentimental ideal of the Nice Dog—a clean-cut fellow who obeyed a few selected commands, was loyal and gentle with his masters, and refrained conscientiously from "bad" behavior as delineated by the same said masters. I had never had one and knew it, and the first dog I owned after years of unsettled existence was the dachshund Watty, who was emphatically not one either.

—JOHN GRAVES, *BLUE AND SOME OTHER DOGS* (1981)

If we lack confidence in ourselves and our relationship
with our dogs, we communicate that to them . . .
in countless subtle and not-so-subtle ways.

—MYRNA MILANI, D.V.M., *DOG SMART* (1997)

"[L]ittle or no reasoning power," I said. "A dog's form of knowledge is: 'This is what we always do.' Change 'always' to 'sometimes' and he'll try to think for himself and you may not like what he thinks."

—GERALD HAMMOND, *THE CURSE OF THE COCKERS* (1993)

Dogs are not evolved to live in a free-for-all structure of anarchy. If they're the alpha, they give orders. If they're not alpha, they take orders.

—BETTY FISHER AND SUZANNE DELZIO,
SO YOUR DOG'S NOT LASSIE (1998)

"Do not lose the leash until you're completely confident of your established bond." "Always say no clearly." "Does size matter?" "One of the dog's favorite games is: where can I hide my big bone?"

—KAREN SALMANSOHN,
*HOW TO MAKE YOUR MAN BEHAVE IN 21 DAYS OR LESS,
USING THE SECRETS OF PROFESSIONAL DOG TRAINERS* (1994)

Cigarette manufacturers, military tacticians, topless waitresses, and dog men training the Delmar Smith way all agree, "It's what's up front that counts."

—BILL TARRANT, *BEST WAY TO TRAIN YOUR GUN DOG* (1977)

Ain't one man out of five thousand gets one-tenth out of what a dog can do for him.

—DELMAR SMITH (B. 1926), BIRD DOG TRAINER

WORKING DOGS

But here, now, was everything I needed, everything I was;
the sled, food, fifteen good friends—or fourteen friends and
Devil, as it happened—all that I had become. I was complete,
and part of that completeness was that we, the team and I,
were in some way doing what we were meant to do.

—GARY PAULSEN, *WINTERDANCE* (1994)

They live to work. They want to pull, herd, guard. They're unhappy if
they don't work. They must do their preordained jobs or go bad—go
sour, get crazy, make your life miserable.

There's joy in work for this group of dogs, splendor in work, fulfill-
ment and devotion and dignity.

The people who write about their working dogs have the same
feelings—they understand the dogs' need because they, too, have the
need.

A small pet is often an excellent companion for
the sick, for long chronic cases especially.
—FLORENCE NIGHTINGALE, *NOTES ON NURSING* [1859]

Their first feat was to carry ninety tons of ammunition to a battery
that was cut off and out of shells and bullets. For two weeks horses and
mules had been trying to get to the soldiers' rescue, without success.
The dogs reached the isolated French battery within four days.
—SHANNON GARST,
SCOTTY ALLAN, KING OF THE DOG-TEAM DRIVERS [1946]

Their tails are high and tongues awag—the
twin banners of sled dog contentment.
—CLARA GERMANI, WRITER AND EDITOR

One sweet female named Tashia, always quiet and soft, was
baring her teeth, taking great mouthfuls of snow and shaking
her head, growling and tearing, trying to jerk the sled loose,
rip the snow loose, tear the world loose and run. Run.

—GARY PAULSEN, *WINTERDANCE* (1994)

The Border collie's natural herding instinct allows it to
handle up to several hundred sheep alone, primarily by
means of a mesmerizing stare known as the "eye."

—JON WINOKUR, *MONDO CANINE* (1991)

With wild range sheep, the herding takes place at
a dead run, a trick not unlike playing chess while
running windsprints through an obstacle course.

—DONALD MCCAIG, *A USEFUL DOG* (2004)

'Tis sweet to hear the honest watch-dog's bark
Bay deep-mouth'd welcome as we draw near home.

—LORD BYRON, "DON JUAN" (1819)

And there it was—the only absolute, the single most important thing,
the be-all and end-all of running dogs on the Iditarod: a tight tug.
I did not understand it yet, did not know how important it would
become; did not realize that I would live for it, die for it, fixate on
it, become totally obsessed with it, eat, sleep, and dream of it.

—GARY PAULSEN, *WINTERDANCE* (1994)

[T]he dog's hard Calvinist heritage where, so long as the
work made sense, life made sense, and outside the work
was death and sorrow and swirling blackness.

—DONALD MCCAIG, *NOP'S HOPE* (1994)

An honest dog will never let you down when you are in difficulties.

—DAVID MCTEIR, SHEEPDOG TRAINER

A sheepdog can work for a man and not give a damn

for him. Must the actor love the director?

—DONALD MCCAIG, *NOP'S HOPE* (1994)

It wasn't just that they wanted to run—there simply wasn't anything
else for them. Everything they were, all the ages since their time
began, the instincts of countless eons of wolves coursing after herds
of bison and caribou were still there, caught in genetic strands,
and they came to the fore and the dogs went berserk with it.

—GARY PAULSEN, *WINTERDANCE* (1994)

These owners routinely turn down offers of a thousand or more
dollars for them, if you believe the stories, as you well may
after watching a pair of scroungy border collies, in response
to a low whistle or a word, run a half-mile up a brush-thick
pasture and bring back seventy-nine Angora wethers and pack
them into a fence corner or a pen for shearing, doctoring, or
loading into a trailer, all while their master picks his teeth.

—JOHN GRAVES, *BLUE AND SOME OTHER DOGS* (1981)

Tugs, pulling, that sweet curve of power from the gangline
and up over their backs became everything—more than
money, love, family—more than life. The tug.

—GARY PAULSEN, *WINTERDANCE* (1994)

And never were dogs or men more faithful than those poor brutes.

—ROBERT E. PEARY, *NORTHWARD OVER THE "GREAT ICE"* (1898)

HOUNDS

For my hounds, I know the language of them.

—IZAAK WALTON, *THE COMPLEAT ANGLER* [1653]

Two kinds of hounds: those who track their quarry and those who run it down. Scent hounds and sight hounds. The scent hounds are the ones who "give voice"—who bay and yodel when they come upon that enticing smell. Sight hounds are graceful racing machines and don't speak.

Man found that chasing down rabbits and deer and other speedy creatures was a lot easier with the help of wolf, and so the partnership was strengthened. Hound devotees love hunting the fox, tracking the man, chasing down the deer—admiring their dogs for their brains and keen abilities. And they set down their feelings so well, so well.

Both of them lifted their noble heads in unison, let forth their wonderful joyous bay, and sang their song to celebrate success.

—VIRGINIA LANIER, *A BRACE OF BLOODHOUNDS* (1997)

Hounds, like all real artists, sing on the smallest possible provocation, but they prefer the night before a hunt because they have not dined, and feel—quite naturally—extremely aesthetic.

—FREDERICK WATSON, *IN THE PINK* (1932)

Oft list'ning how the hounds and horn
Cheerly rouse the slumb'ring morn.

—JOHN MILTON, "L'ALLEGRO" (1645)

O where does faithful Gelert roam
The flower of all his race;
So true, so brave—a lamb at home,
A lion in the chase?

—WILLIAM ROBERT SPENCER, "BETH-GÊLERT" (1800)

[T]hrough hunting hounds, and other dogs living
within the confines of your nunnery, the alms which
should be given to the poor are devoured.

—WILLIAM OF WYKEHAM, BISHOP OF WINCHESTER,
LETTER TO THE NUNS OF ROMSEY ABBEY, HAMPSHIRE (C. 1390)

D'ye ken John Peel with his coat so gay?
D'ye ken John Peel at the break of day?
D'ye ken John Peel when he's far, far away
With his hounds and his horn in the morning?

'Twas the sound of his horn brought me from my bed,
And the cry of his hounds has me ofttimes led,
For Peel's view-hollo would waken the dead,
Or the fox from his lair in the morning.

—JOHN WOODCOCK GRAVES, "D'YE KEN JOHN PEEL?" (1824)

She regarded the pack gravely and remarked, "What a lot of dogs!"
She was corrected. "Those are hounds, darling!" She again studied the
pack, and then said, controversially, "Well, they're very like dogs."

**—EDITH SOMERVILLE, "AN APPRECIATION"
IN *THE SILVER HORN* (1934)**

So what is a racer? It is a dog that runs twice a week at speeds
over 40 mph around an oval track ranging in length from
5/16 to 9/16 of a mile. When it isn't racing, it is sleeping.

—SUSAN OLASKY, *A DOG'S LIFE: RACERS TURNED PETS* (1996)

I do not nowadays go to the circus to see a dog chase a rabbit,
but if by chance I pass such a race, in the fields, it quite
easily distracts me even from some serious thoughts.

—SAINT AUGUSTINE, *CONFESSIONS AND ENCHIRIDION* (397 AD)

[T]heir cry had not the lonesome, wailing, contralto lament that
one may listen to in the Kerry mountains, when the dark hounds
are away in the high places, merged in the darkness of the heather.

—EDITH SOMERVILLE, "AN APPRECIATION,"
IN *THE SILVER HORN* (1934)

My love shall hear the music of my hounds.

Uncouple in the western valley; let them go:

Dispatch, I say, and find the forester.

We will, fair queen up to the mountain's top,

And mark the musical confusion

Of hounds and echo in conjunction.

The skies, the fountains, every region near

Seem'd all one mutual cry: I never heard

So musical a discord, such sweet thunder.

—WILLIAM SHAKESPEARE, *A MIDSUMMER NIGHT'S DREAM* (1605)

In dreams ye choose a prey, and like some hound,

That even in sleep doth ply woodland toil,

Ye bell and bay.

—AESCHYLUS, *EUMENIDES* (458 BC)

[T]hey should be of the superior kind in spirit, in speed, in scent and in hair. In the first place they will show spirit if they do not leave scenting when the stifling heat comes on; and good at scent if they apprehend the hare in bare, dry and sunny localities at the advent of the dog-star, sound of foot if during the same season of the year their feet are not blistered when they run over mountainous grounds. As to the coating of the hair, it should be fine and thick and soft.

—XENOPHON, *CYNEGETICUS* (C. FOURTH CENTURY BC)

For a pack with a sweet cry, he recommended starting "some large dogs that have deep solemn mouths . . . which must as it were bear the bass in the consort, then a double number of roaring, and loud ringing mouths, which bear the counter-tenor, then some hollow plain sweet mouths, which bear the mean or middle part." Finally, he suggests that "amongst these you cast in a couple or two of small singing beagles, which as small trebles may warble amongst them" to provide a balanced symphony.

—GERVASE MARKHAM, *COUNTRY CONTENTMENTS* (1633)

[A] hell-sent hound.

—AESCHYLUS, *PROMETHEUS BOUND* (C. FIFTH CENTURY BC)

A lot of people think that because bloodhounds are used by law enforcement, and cover more ground than other hounds, they're trained to guard and attack. Not true. They are gentle animals.

—VIRGINIA LANIER, *A BRACE OF BLOODHOUNDS* (1997)

All hunting stories are the same, . . . just as all Turf stories are the same.

—H. H. MUNRO (SAKI), *ESME* (1910)

Dog racing is a $4 billion gambling industry . . . attracting 27 million fans to 55 tracks in 18 states. . . . The biggest purse ever was $130,153 offered in a stake race at the Woodlands in Kansas City, Kansas, in 1995.

—SUSAN OLASKY, *A DOG'S LIFE: RACERS TURNED PETS* (1996)

In some countries a hunting parson is no uncommon sight. Such a one might make a good shepherd's dog, but is far from being the Good Shepherd.

—HENRY DAVID THOREAU, *WALDEN* (1854)

SPORTING DOGS

Grouse hunting without a dog is not grouse hunting at all.

—WILLIAM HARNDEN FOSTER,

NEW ENGLAND GROUSE SHOOTING (1942)

Probably dog's first task was to help man to hunt, to find food for both of them. Surely the sporting dogs—spaniels and pointers and all the retrievers—are the highest expression of that task. Finding the game, flushing it for the gun, and then bringing it back—why, all the hunter has to do is fire his gun. And, oh yes, find the right dog and train him and work him and keep him healthy and happy and condition him and . . .

Sometimes hunters write about their dogs and how it feels to work with them in the field. Their comments are deep and heartfelt.

Dogs are natural athletes. The sporting breeds—retrievers, pointers, terriers, spaniels—are after all jocks. They live to do what centuries of selective breeding has equipped them to do best: work out.

—JON WINOKUR, *MONDO CANINE* (1991)

Crisp flushed the final woodcock of the day. We watched it flicker through the reeds in silhouette, and wished it well.

—KENNETH ROEBUCK, *BRONX HOUSE WOODCOCK*

The retriever, whose upraised eyes bulged wider, the dog's ears pricking and its tail brooming the creekbank mud: Soon the falling-leaf shapes of ducks would reflect in those amber orbs.

—C. LEONARD FERGUS, *GUN DOG BREEDS* (1992)

You may hear him breaking a twig, or splashing in a wet spot, or plopping into the creek. But when all sound ceases, be ready for instant action, for he is likely on point.

—ALDO LEOPOLD, *A SAND COUNTY ALMANAC* (1949)

Falling asleep on the gather'd leaves

with my dog and gun by my side.

—WALT WHITMAN, *LEAVES OF GRASS* (1855)

[He is about my age] . . . with the alert and

amused face of certain hunting dogs.

—JEREMY BERNSTEIN, *MOUNTAIN PASSAGES* (1978)

When he hath found the bird, he keepeth sure and fast silence,

he stayeth his steps and will proceed no further and with a

close, covert watching eye, layeth his belly to the ground.

—JOHN CAIUS, *OF ENGLISHE DOGGES* (1576)

After all, what makes a dog a bird dog is what he does about birds.

—HAVILAH BABCOCK, "WHEN A MAN'S THOUGHTS ARE PURE" (1964)

Think and say what you like about me, but if you should
entertain negative thoughts about Buck, I would thank you to
keep them to yourself. If you couldn't find something kind to say
about him I would prefer you said nothing at all and pretended
not to notice his transgressions, which is simply a matter of
good manners when you're out with another man's dog.

—H. G. TAPPLY, "LOVE ME, LOVE MY DOG"

Old gun dogs have stood the test of time and event and circumstance.

—BILL TARRANT, "OF MIRACLES AND MEMORIES" (1995)

[T]hey love well their masters and follow them without
losing, although they be in a great crowd of men, and
commonly they go before their master, running and wagging
their tail, and raise or start fowl and wild beasts.

—GASTON PHOEBUS III, *LIVRE DE CHASSE* (1507)

[H]e'd make a two-mile cast and kill a calf or a pig or anything that crossed his path and go right ahead on and find his birds, and do it all day. All dog, that's what he was. All dog! A smashin', killin', ground-coverin', bird-huntin' fool.

—JOHN TAINTOR FOOTE, *JING* (1936)

A lost retriever dog, with hanging tongue.

—H. G. WELLS, *THE WAR OF THE WORLDS* (1898)

EPITAPHS

[F]or I waited the better part of a lifetime to own a decent dog,

and finally had him, and now don't have him any more.

—JOHN GRAVES, *BLUE AND SOME OTHER DOGS* (1981)

Every dog I've ever owned and lost is still bright in my mind; I can see them and hear them. A dog's death is sad; the friendship, irreplaceable. And yet there is some kind of lesson in how they go—with dignity and grace and no regrets or backward looks.

There are some quotations here that are so true, so touching that I can hardly bear to read them. Even nasty Lord Byron had good words to say about his beloved Boatswain, though he had none for anyone else, it seems.

"That's the trouble with all animals," he thought.
"They're so much shorter lived than us humans, which
means so many partings in one's lifetime."
—A NORTHUMBRIAN GENTLEMAN, *THE OLD MAN HUNTS* (1959)

Not the least hard thing to bear when they go
from us, these quiet friends, is that they carry away
with them so many years of our own lives.
—JOHN GALSWORTHY, *MEMORIES* (1912)

[I]t's not the same. They don't look at me the way you
do. Other dogs only make me miss you more.

—KAREN DOWELL, *COOKING WITH DOGS* (1998)

Where can I go
without my mount
all eager and quick
How will I know
in Thicket ahead
When Body my good
bright dog is dead.

—MAY SWENSON, "QUESTION" (1994)

My dug? If he wes killed, ye'll unnerstaun, I'd murn
as sair as gin they'd killed my brither.
—ROBERT GARIOCH, "THE DUG" (1950)

I went back to the house and sipped tea and thought of when
she was young and there was nothing in front of us but the
iceblink on the horizon, and I hoped wherever dogs go she would
find a lot of good meat and fat and now and then a run.
—GARY PAULSEN, *PUPPIES, DOGS, AND BLUE NORTHERS* (1996)

If only, my dog, you could know
how sad your god is at your death.
—MIGUEL DE UNAMUNO,
"ELEGIA EN LA MUERTE DE UN PERRO" (1905-1906)

Now thou art dead, no eye shall ever see,

For shape and service, Spaniell like to thee.

This shall my love doe, give thy sad death one

Teare, that deserves of me a million.

—ROBERT HERRICK, *HESPERIDES* (1648)

But soon a wonder came to light,

That show's the rogues they lied;

The man recover'd of the bite,

The dog it was that died.

—OLIVER GOLDSMITH, "ELEGY ON THE DEATH OF A MAD DOG" (1776)

Dog that is born of bitch hath but a short time to live, and is full of misery. He cometh up, and is cut down like a flower; he fleeth as if it were a shadow, and never continueth in one stay.

—EVELYN WAUGH, *THE LOVED ONE* (1948)

NEAR THIS SPOT

ARE DEPOSITED THE REMAINS

OF ONE

WHO POSSESSED BEAUTY

WITHOUT VANITY, STRENGTH WITHOUT INSOLENCE,

COURAGE WITHOUT FEROCITY,

AND ALL THE VIRTUES OF MAN

WITHOUT HIS VICES.

THIS PRAISE, WHICH WOULD BE UNMEANING FLATTERY

IF INSCRIBED OVER HUMAN ASHES,

IS BUT A JUST TRIBUTE TO THE MEMORY OF

"BOATSWAIN" A DOG

WHO WAS BORN AT NEWFOUNDLAND,

MAY, 1803

AND DIED AT NEWSTEAD ABBEY

NOV. 18, 1808

—INSCRIPTION ON A GRAVESTONE IN NEWSTEAD ABBEY

Ye, who perchance behold this simple urn,

Pass on—it honors none you wish to mourn.

To mark a friend's remains these stones arise;

I never knew but one—and there he lies.

—LORD BYRON, "EPITAPH TO A DOG" (1808)

Dedicated to the indomitable spirits of the sled dogs that

relayed antitoxin six hundred miles over rough ice across

treacherous waters through arctic blizzards from Nenana

to the relief of stricken Nome in the Winter of 1925,

Endurance Fidelity Intelligence

—INSCRIPTION ON THE STATUE OF BALTO

IN CENTRAL PARK, NEW YORK

Here lies Dash, the Favourite Spaniel of Queen Victoria,

By whose command this Memorial was Erected.

He died on the 20 December, 1840 in his 9th year.

His attachment was without selfishness,

His playfulness without malice.

His fidelity without deceit.

Reader, if you would live beloved and die regretted,

profit by the example of Dash.

—INSCRIPTION ON THE GRAVESTONE OF

QUEEN VICTORIA'S DOG, DASH

INDEX